I want to buy a House, Now What?!™

Chris Sandlund

SILVER
LINING
BOOKS

NEW YORK

Other titles in the Now What?!™ series:
I'm turning on my PC, Now What?!
I'm turning on my iMac, Now What?!
I'm in the Wine Store, Now What?!
I'm in the Kitchen, Now What?!
I need to get in Shape, Now What?!
I need a Job, Now What?!
I haven't saved a Dime, Now What?!
I'm on the Internet, Now What?!
I just bought a Digital Camera, Now What?!
I'm Retiring, Now What?!
I'm getting Married, Now What?!
I've got a Grill, Now What?!
I need to give a Presentation, Now What?!
I want Cosmetic Surgery, Now What?!
I think I need a Lawyer, Now What?!

Titles in the Now What?!™ mini series:
I just got a Handheld Organizer, Now What?!
I just got a Cell Phone, Now What?!

introduction

"Why doesn't anyone tell you how stressful buying a house can be? First the searching, then the endless little details, the indecipherable contracts, the fees. Wow, it gets so complicated!" cried my friend Julie B. "Isn't there help anywhere for all of this?"

Yes, there is—and it's right here in *I want to buy a House, Now What?!* Consider it your inside track on home ownership. This book will walk you through the entire process, from looking to negotiating to redecorating. There are exceedingly useful planning timelines on the buying process (pages 40–41) and the closing process (pages 92–93). These timelines tell you exactly what to do when, so you won't drop the proverbial stitch. You'll also find a wealth of real estate secrets, such as how a low bid can win out (tell the seller you will move to suit his schedule) and what renovations will pay for themselves (improving the kitchen) and which ones won't (adding a pool). And since you never know when you might decide to move, there's even a chapter on selling your house.

Chances are buying a house is the biggest investment of your life. And, yes, it can be scary. But don't let it stress you out! Get as much inside information as you can. Start right here. Your home sweet home is just around the corner.

Barb Chintz
Editorial Director, the *Now What?!*™ Series

table of contents

Starting out

the American dream

Then and now

So you are ready to buy a home. Wonderful. Now what?! Instead of paying rent each month, you will be investing in your home. The resulting **equity** (the current value of your home less the amount you owe on it) becomes a sort of piggy bank that you can borrow against should you ever need money during an emergency, to cover your kids' college educations, or to help you start a business. And here's even better news: Congress lets you deduct a portion of the interest and 100% of the real estate taxes you pay on your home. That can help offset the sometimes eye-popping price of houses these days. The **median price** (the point at which half of the homes cost more and half cost less) for a home in mid-2001 was $146,000 nationally. (In sought-after locations like the San Francisco Bay Area or New York City, the median price can be much higher.) Not surprising is that this substantial sum often represents the largest investment of a person's life.

The first step to achieving your dream house is to define what you want. Does it have three similar-size bedrooms or one enormous master bedroom suite with two smaller bedrooms? Are the bathrooms newly done with top-of-the-line fixtures or equipped with more standard stuff? Does the kitchen have an eat-in area? Is the yard huge or is it a small, stunning garden?

To help you figure this out, start looking at home magazines and clipping pictures of what you like. Create a **scrapbook** or folder of these magazine photos. Heads-up to married folk: Both parties need to do this, especially if you are shopping for your first home. This **house album** will give your real estate agent an idea about the home you want and will provide you with decorating ideas. As always, flexibility helps. The house style you initially ruled out as one you'd never buy may capture your heart because of its perfect family room.

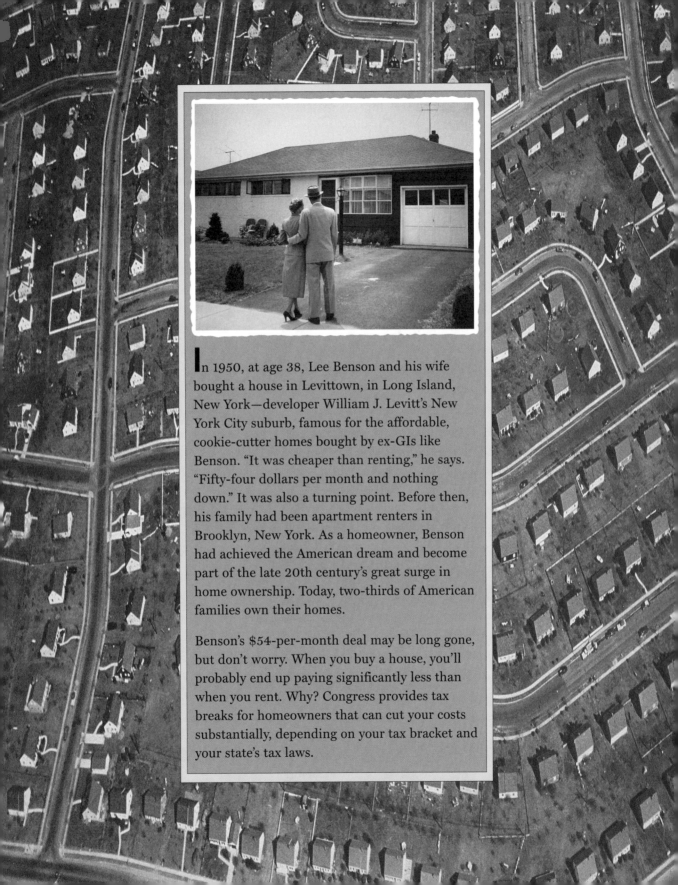

In 1950, at age 38, Lee Benson and his wife bought a house in Levittown, in Long Island, New York—developer William J. Levitt's New York City suburb, famous for the affordable, cookie-cutter homes bought by ex-GIs like Benson. "It was cheaper than renting," he says. "Fifty-four dollars per month and nothing down." It was also a turning point. Before then, his family had been apartment renters in Brooklyn, New York. As a homeowner, Benson had achieved the American dream and become part of the late 20th century's great surge in home ownership. Today, two-thirds of American families own their homes.

Benson's $54-per-month deal may be long gone, but don't worry. When you buy a house, you'll probably end up paying significantly less than when you rent. Why? Congress provides tax breaks for homeowners that can cut your costs substantially, depending on your tax bracket and your state's tax laws.

city, suburb, country

**Green acres
or Park Avenue?**

What are the three most important things to consider when buying a home? Location, location, location—or so the joke goes. But there is a lot of truth to that. Buying a house or a condo is usually the biggest investment of your life. So make sure that you put your money in a well-located home that fits your needs. Consider the pluses and minuses of the big move you're considering:

CITY

Pluses: Cultural events, shopping, proximity of jobs, bustle, short commute
Minuses: Expense, crowding, noise, schools, bustle

SUBURB

Pluses: Shopping, outdoor playgrounds, schools, yard work, more land for your money
Minuses: Commuting, social alienation, reliance on car, yard work

COUNTRY

Pluses: Space, access to nature, privacy, quiet, most land for your money
Minuses: Shopping, few jobs or long commute, quiet

ASK THE EXPERTS

I would like to buy a home in another part of the country. But what if I don't like living there?

Rather than buying a home in some new environment, get to know it first. Start by vacationing there in different seasons, if possible. Consider house or apartment swapping with a local resident who would like to try living in your neck of the woods. The following organizations can help arrange a short- or long-term house swap: HomeLink U.S.A. (800-638-3841; **www. homelink.org**) and HomeExchange (805-898-9660; **www.homeexchange.com**). If you can't house-swap, then try a short-term rental to get the inside skinny on the location. As an insider, you'll learn which local roads get congested during rush hour, where the locals go for lunch, and just how good the local school really is. If you decide you love it, then you can begin house hunting at your own convenience. When it's time to buy a house, you'll be much more likely to find one that fits your desires for years to come.

Virtual house tours

One way to jump-start the home-buying process is to use the Web and go on virtual house tours. There are a couple of paths you can follow. **About.com**'s architecture site has pictures of various home styles that help identify the elements of a home. You can also go to **Realtor.com**, type in a ZIP code and list a few details about your dream house; the site will provide examples of houses—many of which have pictures. Sites such as **homeportfolio.com** teach you about houses' interior details. Print the pictures that you like, or download them to a "House" file on your home computer.

your dream neighborhood

Pay attention to your surroundings

A beautiful house in a bad location does not make for a happy household. That's why thinking about your ideal neighborhood is just as important as envisioning your ideal house. Three key things to consider when analyzing a neighborhood or town are **setting**, **services**, and **society.**

Setting means the proximity of neighbors—including whether you prefer an in-town location or a more suburban one. But you also need to think about your commute.

Before you buy, make sure your new town has the **services** you need; for example, good public schools, a library, local transportation, nearby grocery stores. Remember, though, that many of these will be paid for by your local property taxes.

Finally, consider the people in your prospective new town, or its **society.** Are there lots of kids? No kids for miles? Teenagers? Seniors?

What we like

Americans are deeply divided on what they want in their communities. When *American Demographics* magazine asked what constitutes an ideal neighborhood, here's how people responded:

- 45% said, "A tight-knit place where people look out for each other's kids, hold block parties, etc."

- 40% said, "A place where people know each other's names and say hello now and then, but mostly keep to themselves."

- 13% said, "A place where the closest neighbor is five miles down the road and you see them once a year."

You may think you know what neighborhood you want to live in even before you start looking for a house. Good sources for answers to your questions: your agent, city or town officials, the local librarian, the school guidance counselor, local clergy, the local newspaper, and the owner of the local coffee shop or restaurant.

What's the typical lot size?
An eighth of an acre is small; a half acre is the **median size** (the point at which half of the homes have more and have half less acreage) for American homes; five or more acres is large. A bigger lot size may mean bigger property taxes (see page 34).

Are there zoning laws you need to be aware of?
Some towns have strict **zoning laws** (legal regulations) about such things as running a business out of your home, putting an addition on your house, and parking a recreational vehicle in your driveway. Housing developments also have rules.

What kinds of services are provided for by the town?
Snow removal? Leaf removal? Garbage pickup? Recycling? Recreational sports leagues?

How reliable is the public transportation?
You want to know that public transportation is reliable and on time.

What is the average class size in the elementary school, middle school, and high school?
Class size gives you an idea of how crowded the schools are. Visit the local school and get a tour. Talk to the principal and the PTA.

How close are the shops?
You want a grocery store nearby. Check and see what's available. Is it well stocked? Is it clean and well lighted? Is it always crowded?

What's the typical complaint about the town?
No movie theater, Chinese takeout, video rental, health club? The electricity goes out frequently? There aren't enough good restaurants?

single-family homes

A style to fit anyone's definition of a castle

Even if your dream list specified one architectural style for your ideal home, you should become familiar with the different designs of houses. Keep in mind that the designs illustrated here represent broad categories, which contain many different sub-styles. For information on other types of houses, refer to *A Field Guide to American Houses* by Virginia and Lee McAlester. Or surf over to **architecture.about.com/cs/housestyles**.

GEORGIAN LARGE

Rectangular homes with a central entrance, typically with brick siding. You'll find these designs all over, but especially in the South.

CAPE COD

One-and-a-half-story houses that typically use **dormers** (windows that stick out of a roof) to provide headroom in the second-floor bedrooms. Originally built on Massachusetts's Cape Cod in the 17th century, they became a popular suburban style in the 1940s and 1950s.

COLONIAL

A broad category of styles derived from early New England house designs. Newer versions in suburban developments replace wood **clapboard** (siding) with vinyl or aluminum. Colonials are usually two-story, four-bedroom homes.

RANCH

Based on (what else?) the Western ranch, this single-floor style became widespread in suburban subdivisions starting in the 1950s. Its simple design makes it easy to construct.

RAISED RANCH

These are ranches that have two levels of living space. The staircase is split between the upper level—home to the kitchen, living room, and bedrooms—and the lower level, which is halfway embedded in the ground and houses the garage and family room.

SPLIT-LEVEL

This home has three levels of living space. The top floor is for bedrooms; the middle level for the kitchen, living room, and entrance; and the bottom level (which, like the raised ranch, is halfway underground) is for the family room and garage.

VICTORIAN

A broad category of ornate styles—"Queen Anne" and "Italianate" are a few names you may hear—developed in the late 19th century with elaborate wood carving, dormers, towers, and porches.

TUDOR

Steep roofs and, often, **casement windows** (windows that open on the side like a cabinet). Descriptions include **half-timbering,** which means a wooden framework, often exposed, with the spaces filled in with masonry.

ROW HOUSE/ TOWN HOUSE

Individual homes that share exterior side walls. Each row home has its own entranceway. Parking is usually in a shared lot or on the street. Common in cities, they're increasingly available in suburban developments.

MODERN

Any number of late-20th-century designs based on the stripped-down tenets of modern architecture—for example, with no divisions between rooms.

BUNGALOW/ CRAFTSMAN

One- or one-and-a-half-story American homes of the late 19th to mid-20th century, the bungalow has wide **eaves** (the overhang of the roof from a house's walls) and a porch.

SANTA FE/MISSION

A Southwestern style that mimics the **adobe** (exterior walls covered in stucco with a tile roof) design of the early Spanish missions in California.

new or old?

Sparkling new is nice, but pricey

One crucial decision you will make is whether you want a brand-new or previously owned home. New homes have several advantages: You can be fairly sure that the roof won't leak; that the insulation is sufficient; and the heating, ventilating, and air-conditioning systems (known as **HVAC systems**) are up-to-date. Traditional touches—such as wood kitchen cabinets and pedestal sinks—can even give a new home much of the ambience of an older one.

However, buying an existing home does not banish you to a leaking, drafty house that requires every minute of your weekend for repairs. Your options run from 10-year-old ranches that still feel brand-new to fully renovated old Victorians to **handyman specials** (a euphemism for inexpensive but dilapidated houses), which require tender loving care.

Keep in mind that the median price for an older home (the point at which half of the homes cost more and half cost less) in the spring of 2001 was $146,000—considerably lower than the $172,200 typically spent on a new home. (Both figures can be twice as high in some regions.) Those savings can translate into a lot of paint and Spackle.

Buying a previously owned home can mean moving into an immaculate space, making minor repairs, or undertaking a complete renovation.

ASK THE EXPERTS

Why are new homes more expensive than older ones?

For starters, contractors tend to build for the high end of the market—that's where the profit is. Even in homes with similar features, new houses generally have new appliances and new heating and plumbing systems, most with warranties. That said, you should never assume that everything is in tip-top shape. Even new homes can have problems with termites or water damage. Always insist on an on-site inspection (see page 60).

Why do agents often want to show you new homes first?

Developers lose money if a new home stays vacant too long. In some regions, they may give real estate agents incentives to sell (for example, a higher sales commission). For this reason, some agents will push new-home sales rather than those of existing homes.

Are model homes good examples of what a house in a new development will look like?

If a broker shows you a model home, you need to see the lot where yours will be located. There may be a creek next to it that could cause problems for your future basement or foundation. Ask the agent to show you existing new homes if you have a hard time imagining how your future castle will look on its currently undeveloped lot. Models can also feature expensive upgrades that are not part of the standard package.

I saw a great-looking housing development under construction. What's the first thing I should check?

The first thing you want to check is the developer's reputation. Search online for news stories about the developer. Ask for referrals and talk to people who purchased their new homes from the same developer. Are they happy? Any surprises? Ask town officials the same questions about their experiences with the developer. They may direct you to minutes of meetings where new homeowners complained about the developer.

condos and co-ops

You're all in this together

Not quite ready for a house, but longing for the tax breaks unavailable to renters? **Condominiums** (condos) and **cooperatives** (co-ops) are forms of home ownership—not types of buildings—where owners are responsible for their individual unit or apartment (mortgage, upkeep, and sometimes gas and electric) and also pay a monthly **common charge** (or association dues or community fee) to maintain elevators, hallway carpeting, roofs, and any other shared facilities.

Condos and co-ops are typically either large apartment buildings in the city or attached town houses in the suburbs. Living so close to your neighbors imposes certain obligations. Condos may have pools, but also may restrict your usage late at night. Co-ops may not allow pets.

Co-ops differ from condos in one important way. A co-op is actually a corporation that owns the building. When you "buy" a co-op apartment, you're actually buying shares in the corporation—in exchange for which you receive the lease on the apartment.

Before you can buy a co-op, you have to go before the corporation's board of directors for review. The board will want to see your tax returns and bank statements, as well as letters of recommendation from employers and friends. It's a little like trying to get into a prestigious college.

Condos usually also have a board, but it usually does not have the power to accept or veto applicants: Individual condo owners can sell to whomever they wish. Because of this simpler process, condos are often the easiest choice for first-time home buyers.

What is a loft?

Lofts are units that emphasize wide-open space. Often converted from old warehouses, these living spaces may not have separate, walled-off bedrooms, or, if they do, the walls may not reach up to the often soaring ceilings. Catering to people with artistic flair, lofts often have hardwood floors, exposed brick walls, and exposed ductwork. **Timber lofts** are stylish—they have wood beams—but are often not as soundproof as those built with concrete.

Ⓐsk the experts

Can a condo or co-op bill me for something that goes wrong in the complex but isn't in my unit?

Condos and co-ops will bill you for extraordinary repairs which are not covered by insurance. These repairs, called **special assessments,** typically show up as a separate item in your common charge bill. Ask the seller for information about the condo association or co-op's insurance coverage and how it's managed. Too many "special assessments" means they haven't planned for contingencies.

I'm tired of condo living, but I can't quite afford single-family homes in my area. What should I do?

Consider buying a property that has two to four attached apartments or houses, and living in one of the units. Like a single-family homeowner, you own land and make decisions without needing approval from other owners. If you're ready to be a landlord, the rent you collect from the other units will be extra income.

What is a duplex?

A duplex is simply a place with two levels of living space.

FIRST PERSON DISASTER STORY

RULES TO ABIDE BY

When I bought my condo in Silicon Valley, I was ecstatic. I had purchased a second-floor, sun-drenched apartment overlooking a pool. It cost one-third of what a single-family home would. Several years later, however, I decided to take a new job and move back to Washington, D.C. I didn't want to sell my condo, so I put an ad in the paper to rent it. I found a great tenant and contacted the condo association to tell them I was renting out my unit. Much to my amazement, I was informed that owners could no longer rent their apartments. Hadn't I seen the change in the bylaw memo last year? No, I hadn't. I protested, but there was nothing they could do for me—we all had to abide by the new rules. I was so mad I sold the condo that month and vowed never to buy another one.

—Alice C., Alexandria, Virginia

what can you afford?

It takes a mortgage

Time for a reality check. The biggest obstacle to achieving your dream house is money: How much house can you afford? That depends on three factors: how much cash you have on hand, how big a mortgage the bank is willing to lend you, and—very important—how big a mortgage you can afford.

A **mortgage** works something like the installment plans you may be used to for smaller purchases, such as cars, computers, or appliances. The bank lends you money to buy the house, and you pay off the **principal** of the loan at a set interest rate. The big difference is the amount of money and length of time involved—the average term for a mortgage is 30 years. That extended time frame allows you to afford a much better home than you could if you had to buy it outright, or pay for it over 3, 5, or 10 years.

Don't worry about the details of mortgages and interest rates just yet (see page 78 when you're ready). What you're looking for now is a ballpark figure you can use to keep your house hunting realistic.

Banks want to know that you'll be able to meet the monthly payments for the house reliably. So determine how much money you'll be able to put toward the monthly payments and real estate taxes. (Use the amount of your current rent as a guide.) Conventional wisdom says that your house should cost no more than 2.5 times your income. That means if you make $60,000 a year, you can afford to spend $150,000 to buy a home.

A house often represents the biggest investment of your life.

One-time costs

The old rule of thumb for buying a house was that you should put down at least 10% of the house's sale price yourself, but banks will now let you invest as little as 3%. Depending on how much you do put down, banks will often demand that you purchase **private mortgage insurance** (a policy that guarantees to pay your mortgage if you don't make the payments).

There are literally dozens of other smaller costs—from lawyer's fees to packing supplies. Closing costs alone typically run 2% to 3% of the house's cost. Different cities and states have different real estate practices, so these one-time costs will vary according to region:

Down payment ■ Real estate lawyer ■ House inspector's or engineer's report ■ Deed or title insurance ■ Bank fees at closing ■ Decorating allowance

Month-to-month costs

It's vital to consider your month-to-month costs, which are different depending on the co-op or condo:

Mortgage payments ■ Homeowner's insurance* ■ Property taxes* ■ Utilities ■ Heat ■ Water ■ Garbage removal ■ Pest control ■ Repairs ■ Maintenance*

(*Frequently bundled in your mortgage payment)

Panic Attack

I never imagined these expenses in the first week after closing: $125 to change the locks; $1,000 for outdoor motion detector lights; $1,000 for heavy-duty closet and drawer organizers; $200 for a water filter in the kitchen and to replace missing screens; and $300 for phone jacks. Sheesh! O.K., I'll hold off buying a coffee table and TV.

now what do I do?
Answers to common questions

How can I find out exactly how much I can afford?

There are plenty of sources that will help you out. Several Web sites, including CBS's "MarketWatch," have **free calculators**—pages that ask you questions about your income and debt load, then determine the maximum mortgage you're likely to receive. Banks will also screen you, but they tend to do so as part of a **prequalification** process. Prequalifying can accelerate the purchasing process, but it can also lock you into working with a particular bank at rates that may not be beneficial to you. (See page 46 for more on prequalification.)

Should my dream-house list include only my current requirements?

No. When considering your dream house, be sure to include every possible future contingency. As you look at houses, you'll eventually have to make compromises, but now is not that time. Include space for a home office, should you want to work from home. List a separate room for aging relatives, if you plan on caring for your parents or in-laws. Think about what a home might need if you decide to have children—or what it needs after they leave.

When it comes to my dream house, how big is "big"?

Most four-bedroom homes average 2,500 square feet. If agents or friends ask what you mean by "big," ask them to help you by showing you examples of various sizes. You'll quickly get a sense of the difference between a 2,000- and a 4,000-square-foot house.

I don't have time to look through magazines to create a house file. Is that really such a helpful idea?

Yes, because it should save you time when it comes to actual house hunting. Once you show your broker your album they should be able to narrow down your search considerably. Why should a broker show you old houses when a quick look at your album tells him that you like modern features? Don't forget you can create a virtual Web album too, if that is easier. Just bookmark the houses you like at the various Web sites you've searched. Then print them out to bring with you to broker meetings.

Beyond congestion, are there really many differences between country and suburban living?

First, electrical service is much more sporadic in the country than in suburbs. Sometimes countryside phone companies don't offer the wealth of services—such as voice mail or caller ID—that suburbanites take for granted. Finally, rural shopping is usually much more limited than its suburban cousin—both in variety and in store hours.

Is buying a duplex and renting out one of the units a good way to keep costs down?

Duplexes and other multiple-unit housing provide an extra source of income, but they also have their own special considerations. Buying one turns you into a landlord. You'll want to examine existing leases before buying. Also get a sense of the local rental market and rental laws. One drawback: Duplexes receive different tax treatment. They are considered a business as well as a home. When you decide to sell your house, you'll have to declare profits on the appreciation of the business portion of your home.

NOW WHERE DO I GO?!

CONTACTS

The Department of Housing and Urban Development
www.hud.gov/buying/index.cfm

General information on houses
www.homeportfolio.com

MAGAZINES

Architectural Digest
www.archdigest.com

House & Garden
www.house-and-garden.com

Better Homes and Gardens
www.bhg.com

Nest Magazine
www.nestmagazine.com

BOOKS

100 Questions Every First-Time Home Buyer Should Ask: With Answers from Top Brokers from Around the Country
By Ilyce R. Glink

The Smart Money Guide to Buying a Home
By Flip Kenyon and Heather Kenyon

Tips & Traps When Buying a Condo, Co-op, or Town House
By Robert Irwin

Finding a home

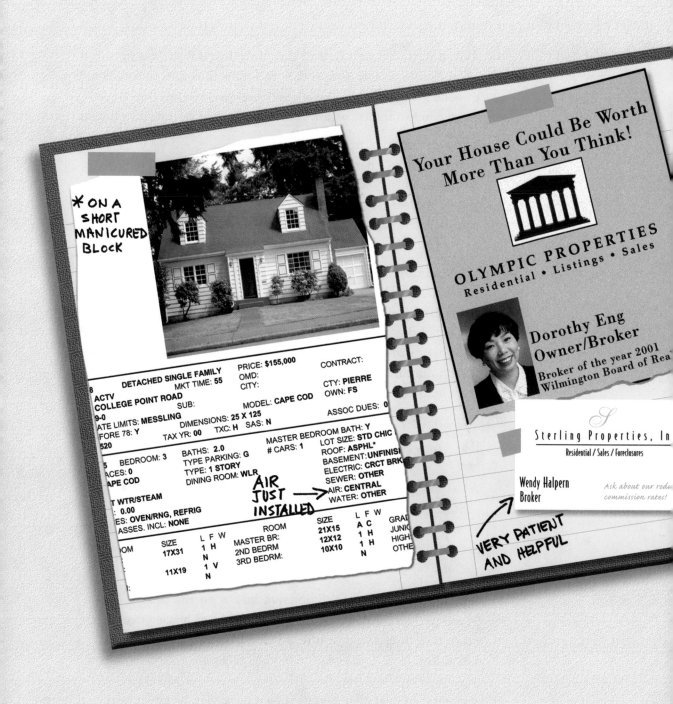

ON A SHORT MANICURED BLOCK

DETACHED SINGLE FAMILY		PRICE: **$155,000**	CONTRACT:
8	**MKT TIME: 55**	OMD:	
ACTV		CITY:	CTY: **PIERRE**
COLLEGE POINT ROAD	SUB:		OWN: **FS**
9-0		MODEL: **CAPE COD**	ASSOC DUES: 0
ATE LIMITS: **MESSLING**	DIMENSIONS: **25 X 125**		
FORE 78: **Y**	TAX YR: **00** TXC: **H** SAS: **N**		

PRICE: **$155,000**

Your House Could Be Worth More Than You Think!

OLYMPIC PROPERTIES
Residential • Listings • Sales

Dorothy Eng
Owner/Broker
Broker of the year 2001
Wilmington Board of Rea

520		MASTER BEDROOM BATH: **Y**
		# CARS: **1** LOT SIZE: **STD CHIC**
5	BEDROOM: **3** BATHS: **2.0**	ROOF: **ASPHL***
ACES: 0	TYPE PARKING: **G**	BASEMENT: **UNFINISH**
APE COD	TYPE: **1 STORY**	ELECTRIC: **CRCT BRK**
	DINING ROOM: **WLR**	SEWER: **OTHER**
T WTR/STEAM		AIR: **CENTRAL**
: 0.00		WATER: **OTHER**
ES: **OVEN/RNG, REFRIG**		
ASSES. INCL: **NONE**		

AIR JUST INSTALLED →

Sterling Properties, In
Residential / Sales / Foreclosures

Wendy Halpern
Broker

Ask about our redu commission rates!

VERY PATIENT AND HELPFUL

		L F W	ROOM	SIZE	L F W	GRAD
OM	SIZE **17X31**	1 H	MASTER BR:	**21X15**	A C	JUNIO
		1 N	2ND BEDRM:	**12X12**	1 H	HIGH
	11X19	1 V	3RD BEDRM:	**10X10**	1 H	OTHE
		N			1 N	

house hunting

Scouting homes becomes your second job

All right, you've got a general idea of the house that you'd like to own. Now it's time to go find it. Spend some time driving or walking through neighborhoods looking at houses that interest you. Write down phone numbers on any "For Sale" signs of homes that you like.

Ask family, friends, and coworkers for their suggestions to expand your search. Tell them some of your criteria, or show them pictures of similar houses (see the section on creating an album, page 8). You'll get ideas for neighborhoods that you may not have considered and—if you're lucky—the inside scoop on houses that are just about to come on the market.

Weekends are the prime time for house hunting. You can check out **open houses** where you can literally walk in off the street and walk through a house for sale. (The real estate agent or owner is always present at these.) Think of open houses as yard sales for houses: They're a great way for buyers to gain some sense of what is available in the current market. Typically, only 10% of the people at an open house are serious buyers.

ASK THE EXPERTS

What are clear signs of trouble in a neighborhood or house?

Steer clear of a house on a busy street. Traffic can make entering or leaving your home a real hassle, to say nothing of the danger it poses to your children or pets. Avoid houses that are too close to fire stations, because the alarms can make for noisy nights and days.

Why not buy the most expensive house on the block?

The problem is that a neighborhood's average house price often determines your home's future worth should you decide to sell it. That's why, ideally, you want to buy the second- or third-most expensive house on the street. Exceptions: Some houses will always sell above the average price because of a unique view or other special quality the others don't have.

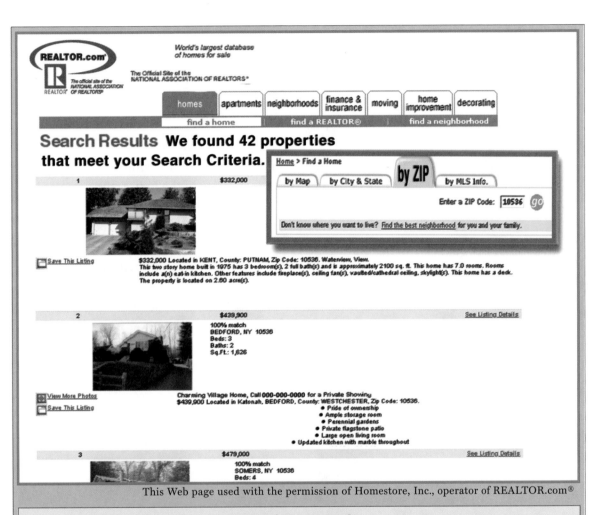

This Web page used with the permission of Homestore, Inc., operator of REALTOR.com®

House hunting online

Another way to house hunt is to use your friendly home computer. Get the ZIP code of the area you are interested in and then go online to www.realtor.com. Type in the ZIP code and you will find scores of homes and their prices. Most come with photos; all come with the name of the real estate agent handling the listing and the agent's contact information. This Web site has access to more than a million houses from across the country because it uses lists from over 850 Multiple Listing Services.

Even if you have to get online access at a public library, do it. House hunting on the Web quickly gives you an idea of what kinds of homes are available in your price range. Make sure you look for Web sites of local agents, which may provide more information.

real estate agents

The go-between

Real estate agents help individuals buy or sell a house. They can help you find houses for sale in your price range and make the search process considerably shorter. Real estate agents can also introduce you to sources for the numerous experts you'll need to complete your purchase, including a mortgage broker, a lawyer, and an inspector or engineer.

For these services, agents charge a **commission**—a fee equal to a certain percentage of the sale price of the house (the commission usually ranges from 4% to 6%). The person selling the house pays the commission, not the buyer. You'll have to be the best judge of your agent's intentions if the agent shows you a home more expensive than your price range. You might suspect it's to reap a higher commission. But it could be because it will include more of what you want. (See "What can you afford?," page 22.)

As a prospective home buyer, you will need to meet with your agent regularly, because the agent will be the one showing you individual properties.

RED FLAG

Beware of agents that represent both the buyer (you) and the seller, known as **dual agency**. In representing the seller, their legal interest is getting the highest price possible. That conflicts with your desire to pay the least. Some states, such as New York, require agents to tell prospective buyers that they represent the seller.

ASK THE EXPERTS

Is an agent's commission negotiable?

Yes, the traditional 4% to 6% commission is not fixed. There is room for negotiation, which can help you and the seller. If you can't afford to pay the seller's minimum asking price, you can ask the seller to ask his agency if it will take a cut in commission so you can get the price you need and the seller gets the return he's seeking. The commission is negotiable up until closing.

What does the term "exclusive listing" mean?

To you, the buyer, nothing much. Your agent can show you a property that is listed exclusively by another agency. Exclusives are a way for sellers' agents to lock in profits and cover expenses by ensuring that they receive no less than half the commission.

Can I work with more than one real estate agent at a time?

You can, but there may not be any real benefit to your doing so as long as you choose an agency that subscribes to a **multiple listing service** (MLS) (see page 32). Because most houses are made available to all brokers on the MLS system, one agent should be able to show you all the houses that meet your criteria. For perhaps the largest investment in your life, it is critical for you to find a full-time, hardworking, ethical, competent, caring agent.

multiple listing service

A cheat sheet to compare houses

Where do agents find out about all those houses? From an ingenious system of listings, known as a multiple listing service (MLS), that provides brokers with details about houses on the market. Nearly all real estate agencies participate in these listing services.

If you are interested in a particular house, your agent will print out an MLS sheet like the one on the opposite page. Here are the important elements to note:

A Picture: Its absence may be a clue that the house is not attractive or it's a brand-new listing.

B MLS Number: A unique identifier of the property in the MLS system. You can look up a property at **Realtor.com** if you see an MLS number listed in an ad.

C List Price: The amount that the seller is asking.

D Address: The exact location of the house, so you can drive by to see it.

E Year Built: The age of the house.

F Taxes and Assessment: Estimated real estate taxes, based on an assessment (or estimate of its value) made in a particular year (see "Local Taxes" on page 34).

G Rooms: Details on the number and type of rooms.

H Utilities: The source of the house's electricity, heating, cooling, and water systems; also indicates how sewage and garbage are handled.

I Schools: Information on the schools in the district (see "Evaluating Schools" on page 36).

J Square Feet: The size of the house, for comparison with other properties (may be an estimate in older homes).

K Remarks: Extra details that make the house special.

A

B 12345678   **DETACHED SINGLE FAMILY**   **C** PRICE: **$155,000**   SALE PRICE: **$0**

STATUS: **ACTV**   MKT TIME: **55**   OMD: CONTRACT: CLOSED:

D AD: **1278 COLLEGE POINT ROAD**   CITY: AREA: **8063**

ZIP: **12345**   SUB: CTY: **PIERRE**   TOWNSHIP: **PIERRE**

CORPORATE LIMITS: **MESSLING**   MODEL: **CAPE COD**   OWN: **FS**   **E** YR BUILT: **1967**

BUILT BEFORE 78: **Y**   DIMENSIONS: **25 X 125**   PIN: **12345612345678**

F TAXES: **1520**   TAX YR: **00**   TXC: **H**   SAS: **N**   ASSOC DUES: **0**   FREQUENCY: **N**

G ROOMS: **5**   BEDROOM: **3**   BATHS: **2.0**   MASTER BEDROOM BATH: **Y**   BASEMENT BATH: **N**

FIREPLACES: **0**   TYPE PARKING: **G**   # CARS: **1**   LOT SIZE: **STD PIER LOT**

STYLE: **CAPE COD**   TYPE: **1 STORY**   ROOF: **ASPHL***   AGENT/INTEREST: **N**

                                DINING ROOM: **WLR**   BASEMENT: **UNFINISHED**

HEAT: **HOT WTR/STEAM**   ELECTRIC: **CRCT BRKRS**

ACREAGE: **0.00**   SEWER: **OTHER**

APPLIANCES: **OVEN/RNG, REFRIG**   **H** AIR: **CENTRAL**

MONTHLY ASSES. INCL: **NONE**   WATER: **OTHER**

ROOM	SIZE	L	F	W	ROOM	SIZE	L	F	W		SCHOOLS	
LIVING RM:	**17X31**	1	H		MASTER BR:	**21X15**	A	C		GRADE:		DIST: **101**
DINING RM:			N		2ND BEDRM	**12X12**	1	H		JUNIOR:		DIST: **101**
KITCHEN:	**11X19**	1	V		3RD BEDRM:	**10X10**	1	H		HIGH:		DIST: **101**
FAMILY RM:			N					N		OTHER:		DIST:

I

J APPROX. SQ. FT: **1700**

POSSESSION: **CLOSING**

REMARKS: **K** **MUST SEE THIS WELL CARED FOR HOME, OFFERS SPACIOUS
LIV/DIN. ROOMS 3 BEDROOMS 2 FULL BATH.
PROFESSIONALLY LANDSCAPED
FULL SECURITY SYSTEM**

DIRECTIONS: **WEST ON OLD COUNTRY ROAD, MAKE A RIGHT ON RT67 AND CONTINUE FOR 1 MILE
MAKE LEFT ON COLLEGE POINT ROAD. HOUSE IS 4TH ON LEFT.**

INFORMATION NOT GUARANTEED, CHECK FLOOD INSURANCE, RM.SZ. ROUNDED TO NEAREST FT.

local taxes

Welcome to the neighborhood

Knowing the vital statistics of a house and even seeing it yourself aren't enough. You need to find out more about the community it's in.

The **MLS sheet** (see page 33) will give you important clues in judging taxes on your property. Obviously, lower estimated taxes mean you'll pay less in taxes. But that's not the whole story.

The **assessment** is the value of the house that your county or state uses as the basis for its tax bill. Generally, assessments run less than the **market value** (the final sale price). In some states, properties are automatically reassessed upon sale. In others, assessed values may not change for years.

Look at the tax year listed on the MLS form. Some towns have yearly assessments, but others wait until a new owner comes on board. If it's been a long time since the property's last assessment, you may be at risk for a new tax assessment—and (yikes!) higher taxes—in the near future. For that reason, ask your agent about the tax-assessment process in your future town.

Note: Your taxes will also rise if your town regularly approves funding school building and other municipal projects. You probably won't mind if you have school-age children; you probably will mind if you don't have children or your children are already grown.

Panic Attack

The house was last assessed in 1970. That can't be right, can it? I mean, that's more than 30 years ago! It's got to be an error. And when it is assessed, will the taxes go up gradually on some kind of scale or all at once? I need to check with the agent.

ASK THE EXPERTS

Wait, I thought buying a house was going to be a tax benefit. Why am I paying property taxes?

The good news is that you're able to deduct the interest you pay on the mortgage for your primary residence and the house's real estate taxes from your federal (and, occasionally, state) taxes. The bad news, of course, is that in order to deduct them, you have to pay them in the first place.

Are utilities considered taxes?

No, they aren't. Even if provided by your municipality, water and (unless you buy a house with a septic tank) sewer costs are not taxes. Still, you're wise to consider these costs as you prepare to buy a house. Ask the seller for several months' water and sewer bills to anticipate this cost.

Tax revolt

Perhaps no issue fans the flames of local politics faster than that of property taxes. During the inflationary 1970s, local governments in California frequently reassessed the value of homes. Citizens who continued living on the same property saw their taxes increase, even though no one voted to raise taxes. Angry, they banded together to pass 1978's famous tax-cutting referendum, **Proposition 13**, which cut back assessed values and locked them in until the sellers moved.

evaluating schools

The cost of a good education

Schools should play a crucial role in your choice of a home even if you don't have children. Why? Few things matter as much to a house's **resale value** as good schools.

If you're still unsure in which neighborhoods you want to look for a home, school-district information can help narrow your choices. Fortunately, there is a wealth of information on the Internet, at the library, in the archives of local newspapers, and through state agencies.

The quality of a school district greatly affects the resale value of a home.

There also are some numbers that can help. Look at statewide test scores or the SAT/ACT average. Pay close attention to student-to-teacher ratios, which give an idea of how much attention students receive. Ratios over 25 students per teacher generally indicate cramped class-rooms and a lack of adequate resources.

Also contact the school district to learn about its computer-to-student ratio, which frequently is not listed in online sources. Finally, check out what classes the school offers. In high school, this means the availability of college-level Advanced Placement courses. For lower grades, ask about the availability of such educational enhancements as music and art.

One-click school data

An **MLS sheet** (see page 33) will tell you the names of the local public schools near a prospective house. With it, you can begin evaluating the individual schools online. Two sources, in particular, will be helpful:

www.theschoolreport.com provides free information on 14,000 schools across the country. You'll get a report on your target school district (or school) and comparisons with others nearby (or your current school). To get this data, you have to provide significant amounts of information to the company—which will then ask whether it can send you targeted advertising.

www.schoolmatch.com works best when you don't have a specific area slated yet. The site lets you choose a metropolitan area, town, or rural district and then find the best schools in the region. If you want more than the name of the school, however, you'll have to pay for a report—which costs $34.

Even with all this information, comparing individual schools is a little like mixing apples and oranges. There are still no nationwide tests for grade schools and middle schools despite recent calls to action. SAT (and, to a lesser degree, ACT) data provide some basis for comparison—but there remains an undercurrent of skepticism as to whether these numbers accurately reflect the overall educational ability of a school.

Childcare

As you investigate houses, be sure to look into childcare options for young children as well as the availability of afterschool programs for older children. Ask your agent, friends, or family for the names of childcare facilities nearby. Or visit the National Network for Child Care's Web site at **www.nncc.org** for more information on how to evaluate childcare options.

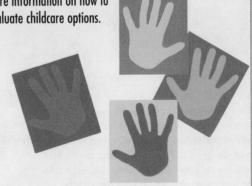

things to look out for

Don't ignore potential problems

Remember that agents are salespeople, and that means they'll highlight the positives. It's up to you to research the negatives.

Among the nastiest negatives is crime. Find out two statistics for a given neighborhood: the number of violent crimes (such as murder, rape, and assault) and property crimes (burglary and auto theft). For this information, you can call the local police precinct or the neighborhood association, and read the local newspaper and police blotter.

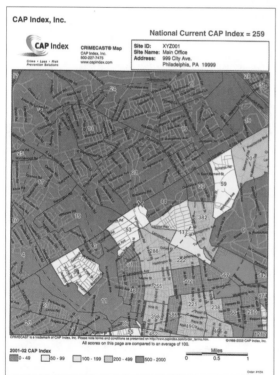

Find crime rates for the neighborhoods where you're house hunting at homeadvisor.msn.com, www.realtor.com, and www.capindex.com. For a fee, you can get a CAP Index site map, shown here, which uses green for low crime risk, yellow for average risk, and red for high crime spots.

Online, Microsoft's HomeAdvisor (**homeadvisor.msn.com**) and Realtor.com (**www.realtor.com**) provide crime ratings for a particular ZIP code. For even more detailed information, contact The CAP Index (**www.capindex.com**)—which sells reports covering a neighborhood's crime risk for a modest fee.

Equally important is a visual evaluation of an area. Does the town collect its trash? Are jungle gyms and other playground equipment in good condition? Do you drive over a lot of potholes?

Finally, there's the problem of traffic. Driving tours give you a chance to evaluate how convenient amenities such as grocery stores, schools, playgrounds, libraries, and public transportation are to a possible home. Visit during rush hour to get a sense of traffic patterns. The best way to research the commute is to get up extra early and drive it one morning or in the evening.

ASK THE EXPERTS

How do I know if the crime level is good or bad?

HomeAdvisor and Realtor.com provide ratings for individual neighborhoods, but places may sound scary with anything less than a perfect score—even though they are perfectly nice neighborhoods. To get a sense of how much crime you consider bad, check the crime data for your current neighborhood. You already have a sense of how safe you feel at home. That number can become your gauge for other areas.

Why do potholes and playgrounds remain decrepit?

Read the local newspaper's coverage of town hall meetings or county board of supervisors meetings. Sometimes your cable television provider will carry these meetings on its community-access channels. If you don't see issues such as road or playground repair being discussed, you know that they won't be settled anytime soon. These observations tell you that the local government may lack the money to make repairs or has its priorities elsewhere—in which case maybe you should be house hunting elsewhere, too.

FIRST PERSON DISASTER STORY

ALLERGIC TO MY HOUSE

My 6-year-old son and I are both highly allergic to cats. All we have to do is be around one and we start sneezing. When my husband's job called for a transfer to another state, we started house hunting. We only had a few weeks to look, so we were thrilled when we found just the right house the first week, and there had been no pets living there. Once we moved in, however, my allergies started acting up again and so did my son's. We figured it was hay fever or something, but it just kept getting worse. I happened to mention it to one of my new neighbors, who wondered if the problem was cat hair. Turns out the owner previous to the woman who sold us the house had had 16 cats! We ended up having to have all the carpets deep-cleaned and the walls washed down, but it did the trick.

—Jennifer W., Miami, Florida

the buying process

The road ahead, from start to finish

How long it takes from thinking about a house to actually buying it depends on you and your region's customs. Hustle through the steps and you might be able to close on a property within three months. More realistically, expect to spend every other weekend for the next six months to find the home of your dreams. Of course, if you have to move quickly, you may not have the luxury of looking around. Either way, here is a brief overview of the home-buying process.

Before you begin looking for a specific house:

- Identify which attributes of a house are important to you.
- Create a scrapbook from magazine and online photos that illustrates details that you want.
- Talk to family and friends about what they like and dislike about their homes.
- Research basic styles of houses and their elements online so you know what an agent is talking about.
- Define the type of neighborhood you want to look in.
- Determine how much you can afford or, better yet, go through a complete mortgage prequalification process (see page 46).

Once you're ready to look at properties:

- Select several areas where you might be comfortable.
- Tour these communities to learn about their shopping opportunities; community services, such as swimming pools or parks; and public transportation links.
- Begin looking at homes in these areas.
- Visit some open houses of homes for sale.
- Narrow your search to two or three neighborhoods.
- Ask friends, family, and coworkers for names of real estate agents. Interview as many as you can. Ask them if they work full time as an agent, what associations they belong to, and how long they have been selling. Ask them: What are the common practices and procedures of buying a home in their area?

- Select an agent, then visit a few properties with her to get a sense of how she works.
- Start hunting for a house, getting the agent to show you as many homes as you can stand.
- Take notes on each home, even the wrecks. Write down the date, address, and outstanding details.

When you have seen a house you're interested in:

- Investigate the schools, either for your own kids or just to make sure the house will retain its resale value. In towns with good public schools, local taxes are typically high. Check to see if local taxes are rising rapidly or due for an increase.
- Visit the house a few times at different hours of the day and night. See how the traffic is at night and on weekends.
- Ask the owner about his utility bills, to get a sense of your likely costs.
- Determine a fair price for the house in the local market and make a bid.

After your bid has been accepted:

- Hire a real estate lawyer.
- Sign a contract with the seller, after having it reviewed by your lawyer.
- Put money down on the house; the seller's attorney will place it in escrow.
- Hire an inspector or engineer to look over the house.

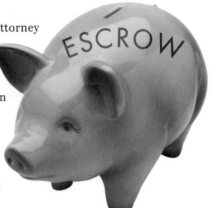

- Negotiate price or contract changes based on the inspector's report; arrange your closing date.
- Secure homeowner's insurance for your new house in order to get your mortgage.
- Obtain a mortgage (see page 80) if you haven't already been preapproved (see page 46).
- Have your lawyer check that the owner has clear title to sell the house.
- Close on the house.

now what do I do?
Answers to common questions

Do I have to use a computer to look for homes?

Newspapers and real estate catalogs cannot reflect up-to-date prices. You may miss a house that you thought was unaffordable if the seller decides to lower the price. You may also spend time looking at properties that have already been sold. Avoiding these aggravations may be worth the effort spent using a computer.

Why is it difficult to find houses that aren't listed with an agent?

Agents are professionals who know all the tricks for listing a house. A homeowner trying to sell a house by himself will frequently overlook essential details—such as not listing the property correctly in the newspaper or neglecting to place an ad online. That's the reason agents earn such a nice commission—and why it's best to turn to them to find the greatest variety of homes.

Is there any way to find out what types of people live in a particular town?

Marketers use something called **psychographics** to describe individuals with common behaviors—such as the outdoor enthusiast or the avid gardener. They're a little horoscope-ish, but they describe individual traits, such as a love of specific television shows, with reasonable accuracy. The marketing firm Claritas provides an online database of psychographics for each ZIP code in the country at **yawyl.claritas.com**. This tool gives you an idea if the people in a town are folks like you.

Are agent commissions the same across the country?

They range from about 4% to 6%. While there may be a common rate in a region, it is illegal for the industry to set one commission rate.

What trouble signs should I look for in a prospective home?

Watch out for cracks, water stains, and termites or other bugs. Also look for leaking underground oil tanks, asbestos, radon (see page 76), illegal additions such as a deck or pool, and lead-based paint on walls (which by federal law should be disclosed). Before you finalize the deal on any new home, it's worth it to hire a professional building inspector who represents you and can look for hidden flaws.

What are the pros and cons of buying directly from an owner without any agents? If the owner doesn't have to pay a commission, will the buyer see the savings in a reduced price for the house?

It depends. A home for sale by an owner may be overpriced, and the owner may be unrealistic and uncooperative when it's time to negotiate. However, a real estate commission is a significant amount of money, so you may see savings in a lower price.

NOW WHERE DO I GO?!

CONTACTS

The National Association of Realtors
www.realtor.com

Microsoft's HomeAdvisor
homeadvisor.msn.com

Claritas' You Are Where You Live
yawyl.claritas.com

School Information:
www.theschoolreport.com
www.schoolmatch.com

National Network for Child Care
www.nncc.org

The CAP Index, Inc.
www.capindex.com

BOOKS

Buyer Beware: Insider Secrets You Need to Know Before Buying Your Home—From Choosing an Agent to Closing the Deal
By Carla Cross

10 Traits of Highly Successful Schools: How You Can Know If Your School Is a Good One
By Elaine K. McEwan

Getting the Best Education for Your Child: A Parent's Checklist
By James Edward Keogh

Getting ready to buy

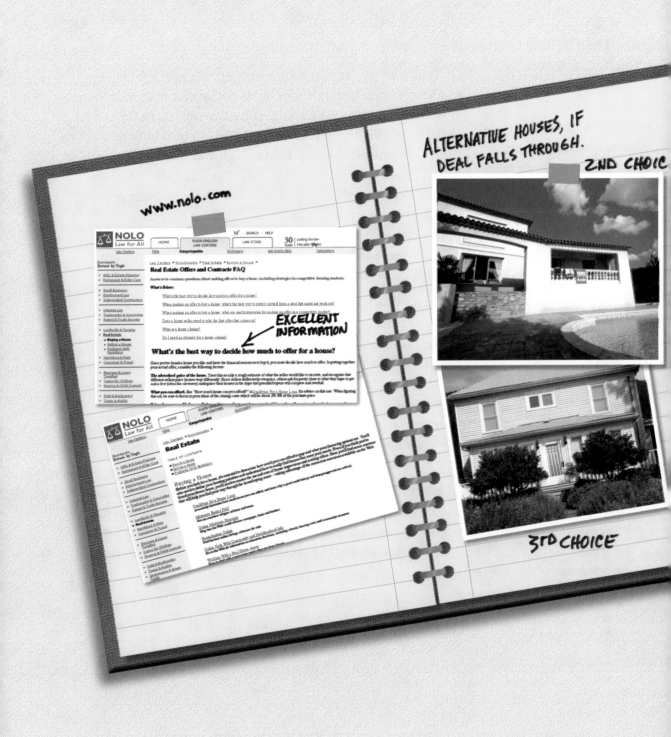

bidding

Get ready to haggle

Prequalification

A seller will accept your offer only if he believes you'll be able to close the deal. You can ease his mind by applying for **prequalification,** or preapproval on a mortgage. Many banks will look over your finances and tell you whether they'll give you a mortgage up to a certain limit if you sign a contract on a property within a set amount of time—generally 90 days. Prequalification gives you a leg up on other bidders by showing your seriousness and financial stability. In some areas, preapprovals are a prerequisite to making an offer (see page 78 for more on mortgages).

You've found a house. You want to make an offer for it. Now it's time to make a **bid.** Your bid is nothing more than an initial offer, the opening salvo in a negotiation over the final price for the home. Bid too low and you may get rejected in favor of another interested buyer. Bid too high and you're taking money out of your own pocket. Most likely the seller will come back with a **counteroffer,** an amount somewhere between your offer and the asking price. It's a bit like haggling over the cost of a new car—only the stakes are much higher. In a tough market, where there are few houses available, the bidding on a great house can even go higher than the asking price.

You need to have some understanding of the current market before placing your bid—one reason to look at as many houses as possible beforehand. You also need to know the **comparable value** of similar houses that have recently sold in the neighborhood. Ask your agent for comparable sales lists for the neighborhood for the past 12 months. You may discover that the owner has seriously underestimated the value of his property. Or you may discover that he's under the delusion that his home is Buckingham Palace.

As a rule, your opening bid should not be less than 90% of the asking price. You'll also want to add contingencies, such as the home's passing an inspection, which if not met will allow you to back out of the deal (for information on inspections, see page 62).

ASK THE EXPERTS

How should I determine my initial bid?

Your agent is one person who can advise you on price. Just keep in mind that the more money you pay, the more she makes. That's why you've got to do market research by seeing as many homes as possible to get a feel for how much comparably sized homes are worth. Friends who live in the area can also give you some idea of a house's value.

Should I let my agent handle the whole process?

These negotiations can be unpleasant and sometimes downright nasty. This is where an agent earns her money. Don't let her make decisions for you, but do let her make the presentation on your behalf. She can handle the possibly contentious discussions so that your dreams don't get sullied.

Do bids ever exceed an asking price?

Yes. If a seller receives multiple bids, he can pit the bidders against one another until he gets more than the asking price. Take this as a sign that the market is overheated. You might want to put your house hunting on hold for a few months until it settles down a bit, or else be prepared to move fast and pay close to the asking price—or more.

Does bidding revolve only around price?

Absolutely not! This is the time to be creative. Sometimes a low bidder who writes a touching letter or otherwise develops a great relationship with the owner can win against higher bidders. Or the seller may need to meet a specific closing date that you can accommodate. Plus, offering more cash for a down payment can give the seller greater comfort that the deal will go through.

Should I bid less if the house has been on the market for a long time?

Definitely. The longer an owner has been trying to sell a house, the more likely he will accept a lower offer. Slow markets are a great time to revisit properties that you thought were too expensive. If they haven't sold after 60 or 90 days, the owner may have marked down the price—making it affordable. At the same time, sometimes a home is on the market for a long time because a stubborn seller refuses to come down in price.

real estate lawyers

Why you need one

Agreeing upon a price doesn't mean that the house is yours. You've got to make everything nice and legal—put the agreement in writing and hand over some good-faith money. In some parts of the country, you'll need a real estate lawyer. In others, you don't need a lawyer, but you can hire an **escrow company** to handle the down payment and money for you.

To complicate matters further, real estate law is often localized not just to states but to cities, and sometimes even to counties. Real estate attorneys navigate you through these minefields, look after your interests, and track the details of your transaction. Most have been through so many closings in their careers that they instantly recognize when the seller's attorney is trying to get away with something fishy.

Your real estate agent, friends, and family are great sources for finding an attorney or an escrow company. (Just don't plan on using the seller's attorney, who obviously has the seller's interest at heart rather than yours.) Ask lawyers for references. You'll want to find out how well an attorney explained the process to clients; if all the attorney did was indicate where to sign, then you need to keep looking.

Use an attorney who has handled a lot of real estate transactions in the area where the home you want to buy is located.

ASK THE EXPERTS

How much should an attorney charge?

Legal fees vary by region. As a rule of thumb, your attorney may charge between $400 and $2,500—a huge range but one that reflects the variety of markets. Once you agree on a fee or rate, you'll want to get it in writing (some states require this). Note that the hourly fee for a paralegal or legal assistant should be lower than the lawyer's fee. And be sure you end up with a real estate specialist.

What questions should I ask potential real estate lawyers?

Ask how many years of experience they have. Ask how many real estate transactions they have been involved in within the area. Ask whether they charge a flat fee or by the hour, and whether expenses are billed separately. Finally, ask what their availability will be during the next few months. Do they take calls after working hours? Will they be doing the work personally, or do paralegals and legal assistants do much of the work?

FIRST PERSON DISASTER STORY

THE SCHEMING ATTORNEY

When we negotiated the purchase of our house, my husband and I pushed hard on the price. It was a wreck, so the sellers eventually accepted 30% less than their asking price. Done deal? So we thought, until they backed out of our deal to get a better price. We were disappointed, but our real estate agent didn't want to lose the commission and decided to investigate exactly why they had backed out. It turned out that the seller's attorney saw our price and outbid us. We found out from the bar association that this was unethical. We wrote the seller's agent that we would report the attorney to the bar association for unethical behavior if they didn't nullify his deal. Surprise, surprise! He withdrew his bid and we got the house.

—**Nancy M., Morristown, New Jersey**

contracts

Up to this point, any agreement you've made with the seller has been on your honor. Once you sign a contract, however, you're putting money on the line.

A **contract** is an agreement between two parties (in this case, you and the seller) to do something (in this case, transfer ownership of the house for a set price). In some parts of the country, this same document is called a **purchase offer.**

In any case, it's a legal, binding document—even if it was written up by your real estate agent, who may not be a lawyer. Once a buyer and the seller sign the document, either one can take the other to court to enforce its provisions. Elements called **contingency clauses** define your obligations and describe situations that can scuttle the deal—such as your inability to secure a mortgage.

Generally, the seller's attorney or agent drafts the contract and sends it to you for review. But in some markets it may be the buyer's attorney who gets the contract rolling. If you receive a contract from the seller, send it to your attorney as soon as you receive it. Include a list of any oral agreements that you made with the owner, such as removal of wall-to-wall carpeting in the house. Your attorney should also review the document to make sure that the contingency clauses don't demand too much of you, or leave the seller with an easy out.

You'll want to propose several **contingencies** (or legal outs) of your own. For example, the sale is off and the contract is automatically cancelled if you can't get a mortgage or your attorney or building inspector uncovers flaws that the seller won't fix.

For your opening offer, as well as for the contract, it's important to understand the difference between **personal property** and **real property.** For example, some appliances or other removable items might be part of the house's allure (such as the dining room chandelier or the deluxe refrigerator) but may not be part of the real property for sale. Your contract should include any appliances and other items you expect to find when you move in.

ASK THE EXPERTS

What is a binder agreement?

Binder agreements are used in some parts of the country as a sort of preliminary agreement before signing the actual contract. The intention is to keep you from changing your mind while you double-check the details. However, these documents provide "wiggle room" for the seller or buyer to back out of the deal until the real contract is signed.

How can I tell whether the contract I've been sent is typical?

You can purchase a standard real estate sales contract at most stationery stores. Reading through a generic one helps you recognize unique aspects of the seller's contract. You'll find sections defining the purchase price and various terms of the sale. If you live in an area where the buyer's attorney draws up the contract, a generic contract may familiarize you with standard terms and prepare you to ask any questions of your own attorney.

Are there any terms I should insist upon?

Direct your attorney to ensure that the closing date—the date on which you complete the deal and take ownership of the house—established in the contract isn't too restrictive. The wording for the date should be approximate ("on or about") rather than specific ("on or before"). That way you've got time to fulfill all your responsibilities once you sign on the dotted line. Avoid a contract that includes a **"time is of the essence" clause** written in by the seller. It could require closing on a certain date and force you to forfeit your right to the house if you don't.

Panic Attack

What if we can't find a home in time after we sell ours? What will we do? Live in a hotel? Yikes, that could cost a fortune! I know, I know, I'll put in a contingency clause about the seller giving us two months to find a house after we sell ours. But who is going to want to wait two months? Okay, I'll make it one month.

deposits and escrow

Money talks

You are so much closer to owning a home now. Signing your name to the contract is the exciting first half of a firm agreement to purchase a house. The other part is your deposit, also known as "good-faith money." This can be a small or a substantial portion of the total price—anywhere from 5% to 10% or more.

Who holds on to all your hard-earned cash? Generally, the seller's real estate agent, escrow company, or attorney takes your check and deposits it in an **escrow account**, where it is inaccessible to either party—until certain conditions are met.

Putting money into escrow binds you to the sale. Under most contracts, sellers' attorneys will turn the deposit over to the sellers if you walk away from the purchase.

ASK THE EXPERTS

What if the seller doesn't have a lawyer, or doesn't want to put the money into escrow?

If the seller doesn't want to put the money into escrow, move on. If the stumbling block is simply the lack of a lawyer, however, you should suggest seeking out a nonattorney escrow service. Some areas don't rely much on lawyers, or you may occasionally run into sellers who are marketing their property themselves and see no need to involve an attorney. Make sure you research independent escrow agents or companies. These firms are often certified by a state authority and can provide you with the assurance that your money isn't going to disappear.

Can I use money from my retirement fund for my deposit?

You can, but it'll cost you plenty unless you've already retired. The government taxes preretirement withdrawals from most retirement plans very heavily. Some advisers recommend taking a loan against the money as a way to avoid the tax penalty. Withdrawals or loans can reduce your future retirement savings, however—so consider these steps carefully and seek other ways to raise the money if you can.

deeds, liens, and covenants

The paper chase

Before you buy a house, make sure that it is clear of any legal deadweight that might come along with it. Various legal snarls can severely hinder your ability to enjoy—or even occupy—a house that you purchase. Your lawyer can take care of most of these details, but you need to understand what it means, in legal terms, to own a house.

You officially own a house when the **deed** for the property—a document recorded with the local government that denotes your **title,** or right to the possession and ownership—states that you are now its rightful owner. If you fail to pay property taxes or miss a mortgage payment, a local government or bank can make a claim—or **lien**—against your title.

For a home buyer, however, the big risk is that the previous owner has done something that caused a lien to be attached to the property. If you were to purchase a property with a local-government property-tax lien attached, you would assume the responsibility for paying the previous owner's overdue tax bill.

That's why you'll need to buy **title insurance** (don't worry, it's a one-time cost). Your lawyer or broker will hire a title insurance company to research the deed, confirm that there are no liens against the property, and take care of any problems if they arise. You should also ask your attorney or broker to investigate whether the home has any **covenants** or restrictions—such as agreements disallowing fences or other constructions—attached to it.

ASK THE EXPERTS

Do covenants have to be obeyed?

Conventional covenants, such as those limiting new construction or preventing owners from operating slaughterhouses or saloons, are perfectly legal and must be obeyed. If old deeds contain discriminatory clauses, they are unconstitutional. Federal equal-housing law makes it illegal to discriminate based on race, religion, sexual orientation, or other similar factors.

What happens if there are outstanding liens against the property?

As long as your deposit is safely stashed in escrow and you've hired a title insurance company, you've got nothing to worry about. Remember that the escrow money can be used as a lever to make sure the previous owner cleans up the mess he made. The bank may even demand that the seller not get a portion of your money until his attorney settles any problems with the property's deed (see page 54).

smart buyer tactics

Achieving the best results and avoiding the worst

Occasionally, a problem can occur during the sale. Prepare yourself for this possibility and you'll meet the challenge with the flexibility you need to get what you want.

Deals generally turn sour in one of three ways. First, the property may turn out to be entangled in legal concerns, such as tax liens or a flawed title. Unfortunately, legal concerns can take some time to correct. Second, the house could have serious physical flaws, such as termites or a leaking septic system. Physical problems are more readily addressed, but they can be costly.

Third, a deal can also go bad if the seller backs out of the sale. Find out why she decided to renege on your agreement, preferably by talking to the listing agent. What you do next depends on where you are in the purchasing process. If you have only an oral agreement, you've got to find out if the price you offered was an issue. She may have received a better offer—in which case you need to decide whether to increase your bid (make a **counteroffer**).

Have you already signed the contract? Ask your attorney to review it. The contract's language may let you force the sale even though the seller wants out of the deal. At this point your blood may be boiling. Let professionals, such as your attorney and agent, handle all the negotiations. Let them earn their money—and win you ownership of your dream house.

RED FLAG

Remember, a contract isn't binding until it has been signed by both the buyer and seller. Just because the buyer has signed the contract doesn't mean the seller can't sell to someone else. Sellers may even send contracts to several buyers at once.

ASK THE EXPERTS

Who should I turn to if the seller reneges on the sale?

An agent is a great asset when a deal goes bad, assuming that he's working for you and doesn't also represent the seller. He's likely to lose money if the deal doesn't work out, so he'll work hard to find out why the owner decided not to go ahead with the sale. Your attorney is an essential contact if you have already signed a contract on the house. She will protect your rights if the owner tries to squirm out of a solid deal.

When is it safe for me to back out of the deal?

You can back out of the deal any time before a contract is signed and a deposit is placed in escrow. After that, your degree of wiggle room depends on what contingencies you included in your contract. Typical terms that allow you to break a deal include your inability to get a mortgage, a poor inspection report, and liens on the property.

What should I do if the seller backs out?

As you look at houses, ask yourself whether there is another property you'd be equally interested in. If you simply must have the house, you can try a higher bid to coax the seller back into the deal. But if that doesn't work, you'll just have to move on to another property.

Is there any way I can be sure about the value of a house?

You can never be totally certain. But in addition to your research, you will also get some insight after the bidding's done. The bank that gives you a mortgage will send an appraiser to evaluate the house's **market value.** This expert compares it with similar homes that have recently sold in the area. You'll pay an appraisal fee for this privilege, but it may help answer your questions about the house's worth.

now what do I do?
Answers to common questions

My neighborhood association has certain covenants. Are they binding?

Covenants are rules adopted by communities to ensure that certain standards are met in a neighborhood (most have to do with aesthetics). For example, a covenant may restrict a homeowner from putting up a satellite dish if it exceeds the association's size limits. If you violate a covenant, your neighborhood association may be able to sue you. Before you do any major improvements, check with your local homeowner's association.

What is zoning all about?

Zoning restrictions, while similar to covenants, are typically less restrictive. Zoning rules are created by local governments to promote or limit certain behaviors in certain areas—to keep businesses and residences separate, for instance, or to encourage manufacturing in a given area. If a property is zoned for both commercial and residential uses, you may find a neighbor running a beauty salon out of her basement—with her customers' cars crowding the street. Alternatively, zoning restrictions can prevent you from running a business out of a home office. If you want to change the restrictions for your home, you can usually ask for a zoning variance from your town's zoning board.

How do I find out about local zoning laws?

Call the county clerk to determine which department has authority over zoning. That department's secretary can help you find out most of what you need to know. You may have to go to its office to find a map detailing local zoning boundaries. Large parts of the county will be zoned for different purposes, which the department's employees can help you decipher. Typically, there is also a zoning codebook.

When would a buyer bid more than the asking price?

If you are in a **seller's market** (when houses are selling fast with lots of interested buyers) then you may need to go above the asking price. In such situations, the seller (or her broker) may call for sealed bids from each prospective buyer. This is basically an auction for a house in which each prospective buyer submits a bid without knowing what the other bidders are offering. The one with the highest sealed bid *usually* gets the house, but your relationship with the seller, closing dates, terms, and qualifications can also be factors.

I am buying a house directly from the owner. What should I do to protect myself?

The seller will most likely supply you with a standard contract of sale, which you should take to your lawyer to review. Now about your deposit: If the seller doesn't have a lawyer, be very careful about how your deposit is handled. See if you can have your deposit held in escrow by your lawyer, or suggest that you use a third-party escrow service. In the absence of an agent, who often reminds her client of what to do when, such as scheduling an inspection and applying for a mortgage, both the buyer and the seller must be attentive to the details of their contract.

NOW WHERE DO I GO?!

CONTACTS

Nolo Press's real estate site
**www.nolo.com/encyclopedia/
re_ency.html**

The 'Lectric Law Library
www.lectlaw.com

The American Bar Association
www.abanet.org/home.html

GE National Directory
of Escrow Companies
**www.geloan.com/advertisers/
escrow.html**

BOOKS

**The 90-Second Lawyer Guide
to Buying Real Estate**
By Robert Irwin and David L. Ganz

**Tips and Traps
When Negotiating Real Estate**
By Robert Irwin

**How to Buy/Sell Your Own Home
Without a Broker or Lawyer: The
National Home Sale and Purchase Kit—
Usable in All 50 States**
By Benji O. Anosike

Inspection

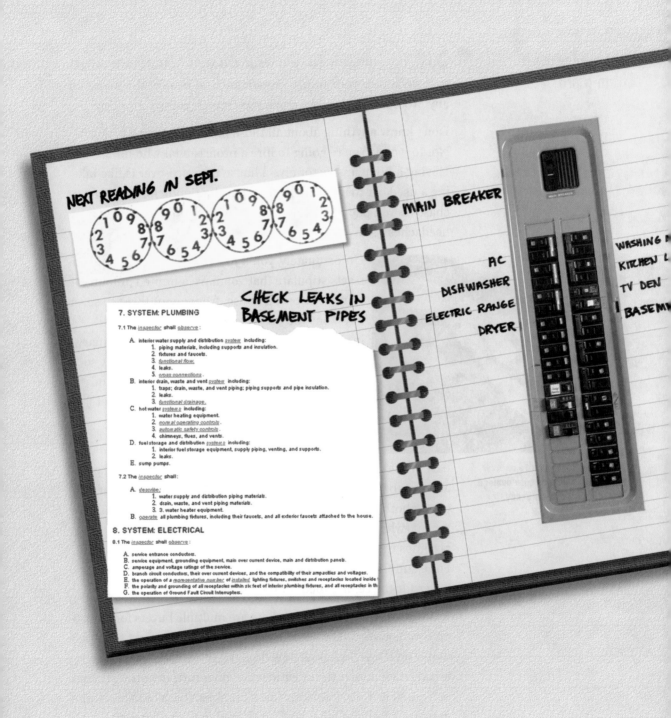

NEXT READING IN SEPT.

CHECK LEAKS IN
BASEMENT PIPES

MAIN BREAKER

AC
DISHWASHER
ELECTRIC RANGE
DRYER

WASHING M
KITCHEN L
TV DEN
BASEM

7. SYSTEM: PLUMBING

7.1 The *inspector* shall *observe*:

A. interior water supply and distribution *system* including:
 1. piping materials, including supports and insulation.
 2. fixtures and faucets.
 3. *functional flow*.
 4. leaks.
 5. *cross connections*.
B. interior drain, waste and vent *system* including:
 1. traps; drain, waste, and vent piping; piping supports and pipe insulation.
 2. leaks.
 3. *functional drainage*.
C. hot water *systems* including:
 1. water heating equipment.
 2. *normal operating controls*.
 3. *automatic safety controls*.
 4. chimneys, flues, and vents.
D. fuel storage and distribution *systems* including:
 1. interior fuel storage equipment, supply piping, venting, and supports.
 2. leaks.
E. sump pumps.

7.2 The *inspector* shall:

A. *describe*:
 1. water supply and distribution piping materials.
 2. drain, waste, and vent piping materials.
 3. 3. water heater equipment.
B. *operate* all plumbing fixtures, including their faucets, and all exterior faucets attached to the house.

8. SYSTEM: ELECTRICAL

8.1 The *inspector* shall *observe*:

A. service entrance conductors.
B. service equipment, grounding equipment, main over current device, main and distribution panels.
C. amperage and voltage ratings of the service.
D. branch circuit conductors, their over current devices, and the compatibility of their ampacities and voltages.
E. the operation of a *representative number* of *installed* lighting fixtures, switches and receptacles located inside t
F. the polarity and grounding of all receptacles within six feet of interior plumbing fixtures, and all receptacles in th
G. the operation of Ground Fault Circuit Interrupters.

hiring an inspector

Get the lowdown from a pro

So you found the house you want. Good for you! Now it's time to really assess your future investment and inspect the house for any problems that might make you second-guess your decision.

Don't know anything about all those pipes, wires, and beams? Not to worry. You're going to hire a professional who does. Having a home inspector give a house the once-over is like taking a used car to a mechanic for an evaluation before you purchase it: You pay a little money now to prevent a lot of headaches later.

Inspectors know how to uncover trouble, including termite damage. They're worth every penny.

Unfortunately, you'll have to move fast. Most contracts stipulate that you have a limited amount of time to inspect a house, from about three to seven days, but you can back out of the deal if the inspection turns up anything out of the ordinary. The seller wants the inspection done quickly so that you can make your decision quickly—and they can get the property back on the market fast if you decline to buy.

Home-inspection fees vary depending on what part of the country you live in, so call a few inspectors and get an idea about the average price before settling on one. Your fee covers both the inspection and the **inspector's report.** This document, which details all the findings, both good and bad, becomes the basis for the final price negotiation on the house. For example, the seller might lower the price to compensate the buyer for the replacement of the furnace.

In a hot seller's market when there are multiple buyers for a property, some buyers take their chances and waive the right to inspection. And if a seller has already dropped the original price during initial negotiations, the seller may not offer further cuts. An exception could be if the inspector finds a problem with hidden termite damage, which the seller is often obliged to pay to correct.

ASK THE EXPERTS

Do I have to hire a professional inspector?

Inspection is one thing you simply cannot do yourself. Only a professional inspector can evaluate the home's condition and find hidden flaws They've checked hundreds of homes before and they know what to look for.

Where can I find an inspector?

The American Society of Home Inspectors (ASHI) maintains a searchable database of its members online at **www.ashi.org.** These professionals have passed a certification test and conducted at least 250 individual inspections. The National Academy of Building Inspection Engineers likewise has a directory of its members, at **www.nabie.org.** Finally, your friends, family, real estate lawyer, and agent are also good sources for references. Get three names, interview the inspectors about their years of experience, and compare prices. You want a professional who knows this business, so be skeptical of a very low price quote.

What should my report include?

When he's done, your inspector will write up his findings in a report. It will detail the structural condition of the house and the life expectancy for its major systems (such as electrical, heating, air conditioning, and plumbing). A no-problems-here report should affirm your decision that this is an excellent house for you to buy. The report is usually a checklist, not a narrative. Checklists are more specific than narratives, which can be vague. Also ask your inspector for home maintenance tips (how often to change the air conditioning and heat filters, clean the gutters, or seal the deck).

electrical

How does a house's electrical system work? Where does its electricity come from? What can go wrong—and how is that possibly dangerous? Here you can learn about your home's electrical system.

Electric meter

Electric meter

The power company's device for monitoring your use of electricity. The meter measures the amount of electricity flowing from the main line to your home. If it's broken, the power company will fix it. It's owned by the power company, which maintains it.

Circuits

These are the lines that carry electricity through the house to the various lights and outlets that need it. The total consumption, measured in amps, of all the electrical devices on an individual circuit cannot exceed the rating for the circuit. Otherwise the breaker or fuse will short-circuit in the service panel.

Dedicated circuits

Devices consuming a lot of power—such as a washing machine, dishwasher, or air-conditioning unit—need dedicated circuits, separate from other systems in the house and from minor appliances in the same room. Otherwise, turning them on and off will make your lights flicker and your computer crash.

Service panel

Also called a fuse box or breaker box, a service panel divvies up the electric company's main line to the various circuits in a house. The total load of a box determines how many **amps**—or units of electricity—are available to divide between these circuits. A 100-amp panel is about the minimum for a modern home, while most new houses include a 200-amp box.

Service panel

Electrical boxes

Verify that all wire splices, light fixtures, receptacles, and other connections are made in an electrical box. This prevents sparks from causing a fire in the recesses behind a house's walls. Boxes should be secured properly to a stud and should not have any dust buildup left from construction projects.

Electrical box

Wiring

Beware of old, rubber-insulated wiring, which deteriorates over time. Check any modified electrical panels and subpanels for safety. Wiring from before the 1920's may have to be replaced to prevent fire damage. Anything installed since the 1960's should generally be fine. Note: It may be difficult to tell if wiring was replaced throughout a house because some old wires may be buried in the walls.

Outlets (also called receptacles)

Determine if the outlets for plugging in appliances accept the third prong for devices that require a grounding plug, such as microwave ovens. Replace older receptacles.

GFCI receptacles

You've seen these—you can recognize them by their red or orange reset buttons. You want to look for ground-fault circuit-interrupter receptacles in bathrooms, kitchens, and garages—especially if you have young children. If water ever hits one, it would instantly stop sending current to connected devices.

Switches

Check that switches move easily from the on to the off position. If they don't, plan on replacing them. Those gummed up by successive layers of paint can usually be cleaned.

Grounding wire and rod

Make sure all the circuits in a house connect via a grounding wire to a grounding rod. That way, sudden surges of electricity will follow a path that safely diffuses them, rather than zapping your appliances.

heating and cooling

Keeping you comfy, winter and summer

A home's heating and cooling systems (collectively known as **HVAC**, which stands for heating, ventilation, and air conditioning) will affect your comfort and your pocketbook. They're also more diverse than electrical or plumbing systems, depending on the age and technology of the systems.

Furnace

Furnace
Determine whether it is heated by gas, oil, or electricity, as well as its age and condition. Remember, replacing a furnace is expensive. Gas and electric-heated hot-air systems are usually reliable; hot-water and steam systems rely on many more components, including boilers, valves, and gauges, each of which can break down.

Conduits
A forced-hot-air system's conduits (the ducts that snake behind your home's walls) usually double for delivery of central air conditioning.

Exhaust for oil- and gas-fired systems
Exhaust should be vented into a chimney or other external outlet. If the exhaust goes through the chimney, make sure it has its own **flue** (an enclosed pipe to conduct smoke) or that any fireplaces sharing the flue are rendered inoperable and used for decorative purposes only. If you're buying an oil-fired home, make sure the owners had the furnace checked and cleaned annually by the oil company. If there is an underground storage tank, have it tested for leaks and determine how much it will cost for cleanup, which can be exorbitant.

Central air conditioning
Newer homes have a central air system which cools air passing over a compressor and blows it through air ducts in the walls and floors into the home.

Filters
Make sure that a hot-air-system's filters— as well as the filters in central and window-unit air conditioners—are clean. Replace these monthly or quarterly, depending on usage.

Water temperature/pressure
In hot water systems, verify that the boiler's water temperature isn't running too hot. Anything too close to boiling (212°F) could indicate a problem in the boiler's gauge. With steam systems, make sure that the pressure isn't too high—which you can identify if the relief valve goes on.

Most homes have centralized systems in which a furnace dishes out heat and a single condenser creates cool air. The three types of central heating systems are **hot water, steam,** and **forced hot air.** It's a good idea to ask to see the records of the heating system's annual inspection.

Thermostat

Thermostats

Modern, programmable thermostats can save you money (for example, by lowering the temperature in the middle of the night and raising it during the day). If you don't have one, check with an HVAC expert, because they're not too expensive to have installed. Most heating and cooling systems divide a house into individual zones, each controlled by its own thermostat. Investigate whether you can adjust the temperature in one section of the house when it's not in use.

Circulating pumps or fans

Older systems might not have these crucial gadgets for increasing efficiency. Make sure that your system has some means of pushing the heat around. If not, budget to get one installed before winter.

ASK THE EXPERTS

How can I gauge the heating and cooling systems' costs?
Ask the owner for two years' worth of the oil (or gas) and electric bills. (Two years lets you average out an unusually mild or severe winter or summer.)

I'm buying an older house that has an ancient HVAC system. What should I look for?
Older homes, additions, and houses in northern climates are more likely to have separate heating or cooling systems—such as window air-conditioning units, electrical baseboard heaters, or woodstoves. Make sure woodstoves are properly connected to a chimney. Watch for paint buildup on radiators, and check that they are placed near windows and doors to counteract cooling from leakage. Window air conditioning and baseboard heating units should be on individual circuits equal to their energy consumption.

plumbing

Water, water everywhere

Plumbing problems can lead to water damage in your home. For that reason, you need to know how your house is plumbed. Where does the water come from? Where does it go?

Main supply line

Standards vary around the country, but the connection from the water main should be at least a 3/4-inch pipe—if not a 1-inch one. A 1/2-inch connection can pinch your supply, reducing water pressure. If the water comes from a well, test its quality. In areas prone to drought, well systems should also have a storage tank for backup (in times of drought, a well may be more likely to run dry or produce very little).

Water meter

The water company regularly reads the meter to bill you for the water you use.

Shutoff valve

There should be a central spot where you can stop all water from entering your home and, should you spring a leak, quickly limit any water damage. There should also be shutoff valves wherever a major appliance or fixture draws water, so you can make repairs without shutting down the entire house.

Water heater

Electrical water heaters are the least energy efficient. Gas is most common for water heaters, but oil-fired furnaces can also heat water while heating your house and thereby reduce your bill. In any case, make sure the heater has an insulation jacket to keep costs down.

Pipes for branch lines

Does all the piping meet local code? Some owners will skimp on repairs or additions by using plastic pipes that aren't allowed in building codes. Older homes may have cast-iron pipes that are corroded badly inside, limiting water flow. Lead pipes will need to be removed for health reasons.

Water meter

Waste vent stack

This is a vent that prevents a vacuum from building up in a home's waste lines. If water doesn't drain well from a toilet or from a full sink, there may be a clogged **stack**—the large pipe that takes away the waste water. You may need to hire a plumber to check this out.

Sewer line

Determine if you have a municipal sewer system or a **septic tank** (a reservoir that holds waste for an individual home and usually needs to be drained by a septic removal company every few years) and a **leach field** (a system of pipes that scatters waste underneath your yard). Sewer lines will generally be O.K., but verify that septic tanks aren't full and that no structures have been built too near a leach field. You may be able to get records from the seller to see how frequently the septic tank was pumped out. Inspectors will typically run the water for an hour or so to simultaneously test the well production, the water pressure, and the septic tank's ability to dispose of waste.

FIRST PERSON DISASTER STORY

THE UNEXPECTED LEAK

When our inspector told us that the roof of the house we wanted to buy had recently been replaced and would last at least 15 years, we thought that we wouldn't have to worry about it. Two years later, the roof developed a serious leak when an early winter snow melted. It turned out that the newly replaced roof covered only that part of the house that had been renovated. The roof over the unrenovated part was 38 years old. No wonder it was leaking! Our inspector should have been more attentive to the two different roofs—I guess he just took the word of the seller and didn't check. Fortunately, I found the source of the leak and quickly patched up the asphalt shingles. That will hold us until spring, when we'll have to replace the old part of the roof.

—Martin W., Rocky River, Ohio

foundations

Cement, concrete, slate, and asphalt

Now you've got to assess the house's foundation. In the South and West, you'll frequently find concrete slab foundations—four inches minimum of concrete on top of a base of compacted dirt, gravel, sand, and a vapor and radon barrier. In the East and Midwest, you're more likely to find a house resting on a dug-out basement with rock or concrete walls and a concrete floor. The two main problem signs are the same for each type of foundation: cracks and leaks.

Cracks may indicate that the concrete, brick, or rock wasn't set properly in the ground and is settling (when the house sinks or shifts slowly into the earth) poorly. Cracks below can lead to cracks in the walls above. A good inspector will help you decide whether to be concerned.

Water stains on the basement floor (or slab) or on walls indicate that the drainage around the foundation isn't sufficient—and may also cause future settling. One source of **leaks** is basement masonry, which is either cement block, brick, or stone. The bonding material that fills the gaps between the bricks or stones, called **pointing**, can erode so much that soil pokes through. That makes an easy entrance for insects or rodents. It's fixable, however, so consider adding these corrections to your list of home improvements you want the seller to take care of before you buy.

Even if you don't spot any water stains, you need to check **drainage.** You want water to drain away from the home to prevent problems. Basements should have a drain somewhere on the floor to let out any standing water.

Panic Attack

What will we do with the new house's unfinished basement? Make a kids' play room? Can we add baseboard heat and a bathroom? I know! I'll ask the inspector what's involved.

ASK THE EXPERTS

Is there any way to get water out of a basement?

The ideal solution is a sump pump. Unfortunately, it needs somewhere to put all that water—which can either be in a sump pit or in your community's storm sewer. The latter approach is better because it's generally less costly, but you'll need to check whether your community's regulations allow sump pumps to be connected to the community sewer.

Sump pump

Should I be concerned that beams in the basement are propping up the house?

Not necessarily. If properly installed, beams and other braces may indicate that someone else has already tackled a major problem in the house.

Should I be cautious about a freshly painted basement floor?

Yes. A fresh coat of battleship gray is a good sign that the owner is trying to hide water stains. Look for telltale signs of water problems, such as rust on the bottom of the furnace or wood rot on the basement stairs.

Can a sealant keep water out of a basement?

To a certain degree, yes. But you have to remember that sealant just prevents water from entering in one spot (such as a wall). The water is still there in the masonry, moving down with the force of gravity. The only way to keep water out of your masonry is to excavate and treat the exterior walls of your basement. As you might imagine, it's not exactly inexpensive and can cost $15,000 or more.

roofs

A shipshape way to top off your home

Your inspector will check the flashing—the metal edge at the joints of the roof and chimney where water can seep into a house.

Your inspector needs to check the age and condition of the material of the roof. Pitched roofs are generally covered with a shingle of asphalt, wood, clay, or slate. A visual inspection from the outside and a peek in the eaves of the attic indicates whether the roof leaks.

Your inspector will also check the **flashing**—metal at the joints of the roof and vertical surfaces, such as the walls and chimneys. These edges are a crucial point where water can seep into a house. If they require patching or replacing, you need to know their status.

Get an estimate of how many years it will be before you'll need to replace the roof. You'll want this information for budgeting and making decisions about replacement materials. Slate, for example, is extremely expensive to replace, but lasts for decades. Asphalt costs less, but wears out more quickly.

Finally, check out where all that water goes: the gutters. These should not allow any rain (or snowmelt) to form puddles. Make an inspection during a rainstorm or just after one to check for leaks in the gutter's seams. Also look for slipshod maintenance. Leaf dams in the gutters can cause mini-lakes that overflow onto a house's **fascia boards** (the boards behind the gutter)—causing them to warp or rot. The **downspouts** (vertical pipes) should carry the water from the gutter to the ground and disperse it away from your foundation.

ASK THE EXPERTS

Does it matter what material my roof is made of?

The tar and synthetic materials used on flat roofs can tear easily. They're easy to repair, but require careful inspection. Slate lasts for decades; asphalt wears out more quickly. Roof fasteners may be nails or staples, but nails are better because staples can cause leaks.

The roof of the house we want seems to sag significantly. Is that a problem?

The house may have a structural weakness. Have your inspector check to see if a **joist** (small timbers or metal beams that support a floor or ceiling) was removed during a renovation, or if a roofer may have overloaded it by putting a layer of shingles over an existing one. Bracing or other engineering remedial work can usually solve these problems. In any case, make sure that your inspector gives you an O.K. before you buy a house with an undulating roofline.

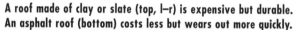
A roof made of clay or slate (top, l–r) is expensive but durable.
An asphalt roof (bottom) costs less but wears out more quickly.

bugs and rodents

Critters can annoy and damage

Nothing else quite spikes the yuck meter the way pests do. Finding out whether your prospective home has bugs or rodents is relatively easy. During the inspection, your examiner should scan the recesses of the house for these vermin. Pests will have left their calling cards—such as droppings or chewed up food—telling you they've already found a home.

Some bugs can cause serious structural damage. The primary culprit is the termite—although carpenter ants and other insects can also cause problems. Should your inspection suggest that there is evidence of past termite damage, make sure to call in an exterminator to verify the home's condition. (Your lender will insist on it.) Termites can eat into your budget as fast as they bore into wood.

In most cases, an exterminator can remove pests with relative ease. But make sure you ask how bugs or mice might have gotten there in the first place. The inspector should be able to point out cracks in the foundation or unsealed holes—such as an outside water faucet or a drying machine vent—that can easily be sealed to prevent further infestations.

These magnified images of termites will help you distinguish them from ants and other pests.

ASK THE EXPERTS

If the inspection doesn't reveal anything, is there any other way to find out about a house's pest problems?

If the owner claims that he has had a pest-maintenance plan for the past few years, verify it. Ask him for copies of the pest-control-service bills and call the service to ask about any recent problems. They'll probably be more forthcoming if you tell them that you're planning to continue using their service after buying the house.

How much will it cost me to hire an exterminator?

Using an exterminator may cost you a few hundred dollars before you move in, but that investment will make you feel more secure. For a longer-term solution, hire a pest-protection service to monitor your home after you buy the house. National firms or local exterminators offer various plans. Most cost less if you have no existing termite damage. Get at least three proposals by checking out the referral service of the National Pest Management Association (**www.pestworld.com,** 703-573-8330). Costs vary widely by region, as does the necessity. Parts of the extreme northern United States—particularly upper New England and the northern Great Plains—lie beyond termites' range. Make sure you need the protection before you pay for the service.

now what do I do?
Answers to common questions

What if I find a problem after I buy the house?

In some parts of the country, your sale contract can stipulate that the escrow money not be released until 30 days after the sale. The escrow funds can pay for new repairs you discover as well as enforce conditions that you included in the contract—for example, hiring a roofer to fix a leak or a carting company to remove trash left by the seller. If that's not an option, and as long as the house is well within your means, you can ask for a larger mortgage than you need. You can use the extra cash that you get from the bank to pay for the repairs.

What if I don't understand something in the inspection report or it doesn't include something I recall the inspector pointing out?

Call your inspector and ask him to go over the report in detail. If there are a significant number of items that he feels should be fixed, ask him to attach a priority to each so you can plan for any repairs. If he's left out something you remember from the inspection, remind him of the off-the-cuff conversation. After you jar his memory, ask for a written appendix detailing the extra item.

Can the inspection cover things not included in this chapter?

An inspection can cover just about anything you consider important enough to have included in your contract as grounds for backing out of the deal. These can range from excessive **radon gas** (a naturally occurring radioactive element that can be cancerous) to lead paint to buried, seeping oil tanks. A good inspector will look for things that do not meet local codes. Check appliances that are part of the deal, such as washers or dryers. Check to see how many **smoke detectors** there are and where they are placed. Negotiate to have as many of your concerns addressed as possible.

How much should I budget for annual house repairs?

In 1997, when the Census Bureau conducted its American Housing Survey, most homeowners didn't pay more than $589 per year for repairs and maintenance. In addition, only 5% of homes required repairs or maintenance that year. If you can sock away $600 in a rainy-day repair fund, you'll probably be in good shape for future repairs.

If my inspection is in July, how can I tell the heating system works?

For any furnace-based system, have your inspector fire it up for a couple of hours. Feel the radiators or place your hand over the vents. You should be able to feel the heat—even on the warmest of days.

Can my inspector tell whether it's possible to reduce the house's energy cost?

Together, you can check for potential cost-saving improvements. Ask your inspector to investigate the insulation around windows and doors, as well as in the attic, basement, and crawl spaces. If there's room for improvement, plan on insulating before winter winds howl or summer heat sizzles.

What's the difference between an inspector and an engineer?

Engineers have to pass four years of college education in addition to other requirements (which is reflected in their higher fees). That doesn't mean an inspector without an engineering degree can't make a solid assessment of a house, but if they find structural damage, they may suggest consulting an engineer. Inspections may also require experts in septic engineering or oil-tank testing. The National Academy of Building Inspection Engineers suggests that's why you may want to start with an engineer in the first place—but you'll have to decide whether it's worth the cost difference.

NOW WHERE DO I GO?!

CONTACTS

The American Society of Home Inspectors
800-743-2744
www.ashi.org

The National Academy
of Building Inspection Engineers
800-294-7729
www.nabie.org

National Society of Professional Engineers
703-684-2800
www.nspe.org

InspectAmerica Engineering, P.C.
914-682-9090
www.inspectamerica.com

The U.S. Environmental Protection Agency
Home Buyer's and Seller's Guide to Radon
**www.epa.gov/iaq/radon/pubs/
hmbyguid.html**

BOOKS

Complete Book of Home Inspection
By Norman Becker

A Carpenter's Advice on Buying a Home
By Greg Evans

**A Safe Haven? A Homeownership Guide
to Assessing Environmental Hazards**
By Todd A. Schultze

Mortgages/closing

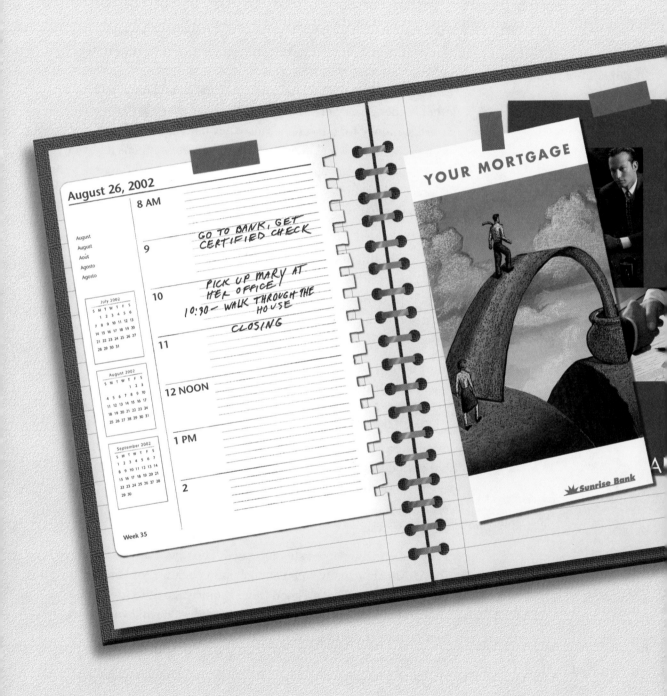

types of mortgages

Fixed and adjustable rates

You've finally found the house. To pay for it, you turn to your carefully accumulated savings and—thank heavens!—something called a **mortgage.** This is a loan a mortgage company, bank, or other lender gives you to help buy the house. Most lenders will approve money for a house because they use the house itself to **secure the loan,** which means that if the worst happens and you can't make your mortgage payments, the lender is confident it can recover its money by selling your home. Your next goal: Find a company that will lend you the money at a low **interest rate**—how much it costs to borrow money from a lender.

How much difference does the interest rate make? Consider this: The monthly payment for a 30-year, $141,620 mortgage at 8.5% is $1,088.94, but just $895.13 at 6.5%. Do your best to pay attention to the business news—mortgage rates can fluctuate based on good or bad financial news.

Most homeowners want fixed-rate mortgages, which means that the interest rate remains the same throughout the life of the loan. But if interest rates are high and you're determined to buy a home, take a look at **adjustable-rate mortgages** (ARM's). For example, a "one year" ARM would have a fixed rate for the initial period (the first year), then adjust upward or downward at each annual anniversary, according to the then prevailing interest rate. A "3/1" ARM is fixed for three years, then adjusts annually thereafter.

Why get an adjustable-rate mortgage? The initial interest rates for ARM's are usually 2 percentage points below those of 30-year mortgages. That's a good thing if mortgage rates are high. And should they fall (which is what you hope) during your short lock-in period, you can **refinance** the house at a low, fixed 30-year mortgage before your lender boosts your rate (see page 94 on refinancing).

ASK THE EXPERTS

What is a "balloon mortgage"?

A **balloon mortgage** lets you pay the interest (but only the interest) on your mortgage at a fixed, low rate for a given period of time—perhaps as long as 10 years. But at the end of the loan term, you must repay the entire principal of the loan. Most people who get a balloon mortgage never actually intend to repay the loan; instead, they hope to refinance when the term is up (see page 94 for more on refinancing). This is a dangerous game which should be avoided, because you might wind up with a higher rate or, worse, have to sell your home if the balloon comes due and unforeseen circumstances make you ineligible to refinance. If you want a low initial rate, consider a longer-term, adjustable-rate mortgage instead (see page 80).

Working around fluctuating rates

Interest rates move up and down constantly, much to prospective homeowners' consternation. Higher inflation drives rates up. Low rates spur more buying, but the increased demand may, in turn, drive rates back up. Rates can even move dramatically in the approximately three months it takes from signing your mortgage application to your closing, drastically affecting the cost of the house.

To provide some stability, lenders allow customers to **lock in** their rates for a limited amount of time, generally 90 days. They haven't guaranteed that they'll loan you the money, just that they'll provide it to you at a set rate if you qualify for the loan.

Follow the news and financial pages to see which way rates are moving, but remember that even the experts can be wrong. If conventional wisdom says that rates will rise, you should probably lock in your rate now. Falling rates make for tempting cost-saving opportunities, but trying to determine whether rates will be lower next week or the week after is a very risky venture. If you're comfortable with the rate, lock it in now; don't get greedy.

running the numbers

Think like a lender

Banks and other lenders will lend you money only if they believe you can repay it. When you apply for a mortgage, they will pick apart your financial life, assessing your credit history, income, and debt. Lenders want to know whether you can meet the monthly payment on the mortgage you've applied for. They'll start by dividing your financial life into **assets** (things you own, such as money or cars, or monies that are due to you) and **liabilities** (obligations that you must pay on a regular basis, such as car payments). For most people buying their first home, their biggest asset will be their **income**—generally a salary, but also any alimony, child-support payments, or trust-fund disbursements). Lenders will also count any savings, including the cash used for the deposit, retirement funds, and hard assets such as your car or other valuables that could be sold for cash.

Too many liabilities for debt, however, will sink your application. Add up the balances on your credit cards, any personal loans you might have taken out (say, for a vacation), auto loans, and student loans—not to mention alimony or child-support payments. Throw on top of that the proposed mortgage, property tax, insurance, and maintenance fees. Now you have a snapshot of your **total proposed debt burden.** If this amount is more than 36% of your income, you'll probably be rejected by the lender. Check out the worksheet at **www.loghomeliving.com** (shown on the next page) for an idea of how you will fare.

Again, the key factor is how much the house will cost as a percentage of your income. Although lenders will loan you up to 97% of the value of a house, they won't do so if the monthly cost of the property alone exceeds 25% of your monthly income. (Though if your deposit is more than 10% of the value of the house, your lender may push this limit to 28%.)

To see how much house you can afford to buy, go online at **www.loghomeliving.com** and check out their worksheets (see opposite page). You can also try **www.housense.com**.

Mortgage Qualification Worksheet

There are two home mortgage qualification tests that mortgage lenders generally make to determine how much money they will lend to a homebuyer. The following worksheet is designed to allow you to conduct these tests in the privacy of your home so you'll know approximately what amount loan you can obtain. Obviously, there are many other factors that lenders use to determine how much they will lend to individual borrowers, therefore, use this worksheet as a guide to your borrowing ability.

The first test is the "Income to Mortgage Expense Ratio." Most mortgage lenders will only allow 28% of family income to be used for home mortgage expense.

The second test is the "Debt to Income Ratio." Lenders generally want total long-term debt payments to be less than 36% of family income.

Income to Mortgage Expense Ratio   **Per Month**
Income
1. Husband's gross monthly income $_____
2. Wife's gross monthly income $_____
3. Other sources of income $_____
4. Total family income: (add lines 1 through 3) $_____
5. Multiply line 4 by mortgage industry's standard income to   _____(x .28)_____ mortgage expense ratio: (28% of total monthly income)
6. Maximum monthly mortgage expense: $_____

Debt to Income Ratio
7. Total monthly income: (line 4 above) $_____
8. Multiply line 7 by mortgage industry's standard debt to income _____(x .36)_____ ratio: (36% of total monthly income)
9. Maximum monthly installment debt: $_____

Installment Debt Calculations
Include all debts that require payments for six or more months after the date of closing on your new home.

Expenses
10. Automobile payments: $_____
11. Other payments: (list below) $_____
_____ $_____
_____ $_____
_____ $_____

12. Maximum monthly mortgage payment: (from line 6 above) $_____
13. Total lines 10, 11, 12. This is your monthly installment debt$_____

Compare the amounts from line 9 and line 13. If line 13 is more than the maximum allowable monthly installment debt shown on line 9, you'll need to find a way to reduce your current installment debt.

Monthly Mortgage Expense Calculator
Mortgage payments include charges for: (a) principal, (b) interest, (c) property tax and (d) hazard insurance (known as PITI). However, most mortgage amortization schedules only include the cost of principal and interest payments. Therefore, you must add the cost of property tax, hazard insurance and mortgage insurance (when required) to determine your total monthly mortgage payment.

The following worksheet will enable you to work backwards to calculate the principal and interest payments from your maximum total monthly mortgage payment.

14. Maximum monthly mortgage expense: $_____ (line 6 or adjusted amount from installment debt, line 13)
15. Permanent mortgage insurance $_____
16. Property tax $_____
17. Hazard insurance $_____
18. Total lines 15, 16, 17 $_____
19. Subtract line 18 from line 14. $_____ This is the principal and interest portion of mortgage.

Using a mortgage table and the interest rate banks in your area are offering, locate the amount determined above (line 19). When you find a monthly payment that corresponds approximately to this amount, move to the column on the extreme left of the chart to determine the loan amount.

Source: **www.loghomeliving.com**

checking your credit record

They've been watching you for some time now

Three companies—Experian, Equifax, and TransUnion—watch the financial lives of almost every American. They note the balance on your credit cards, whether you pay the electric company on time, and the status of any remaining student loans. Even if you finished paying off a credit card, they'll know if you missed several months' payments three years ago. And they sell this information to lenders.

If this sounds a little Orwellian, it is. But Congress requires that these companies let you view the information that they have about you. Each service charges a fee for you to view your report.

It's a good idea to contact all three credit agencies and review your report before applying for a mortgage, as each service may have slightly different information. The reports read like an SAT score, with a final grade given as a number between 300 and 850. The higher your score (called a FICO score), the better your chance of getting a low interest rate.

If you find out there are errors, you'll want to correct them before you apply for a mortgage. For instance, a credit-card company may have sent you a credit card you promptly cut up, but nevertheless still appears on your credit report. (If so, contact the card issuer and ask that they close the account. Then call the credit agency and ask that they remove the card from your record.) Make sure that all the information on your credit reports is correct. Even if the services reject your dispute over an item, they will still allow you to submit a short written explanation of the discrepancy, which they will append to future reports.

ASK THE EXPERTS

What if I bounced a check last year?

You can generally explain a single bounced check to the lender in a letter. If you have good credit and that's your only blemish, you'll be fine.

Should I use one of those companies that claims it can clean up my credit?

No. These companies can't do anything that you can't do yourself. Worse, many are scam artists. You're better off checking with the credit-rating agencies yourself and correcting any inaccuracies. Each of the agencies also provides basic information on how to improve your credit rating. For more help, contact a not-for-profit credit counselor at Consumer Credit Counseling Services (800-547-5005).

FIRST PERSON DISASTER STORY

TOO MUCH CREDIT

I was stunned when my bank turned me down for a mortgage. I was always on time with my bills—I'd never had a late payment. The bank manager suggested I contact a credit-report agency and find out what the problem was. It turns out I had several open accounts from those store credit cards—the ones that offer you a 10% discount on whatever you buy the first time you use it. I had paid the bills and never used the cards again—but I didn't cancel the cards. According to the bank, I had too much ready credit at my disposal, so they denied me a mortgage. All I had to do was cancel the cards and I was back in business. I did it, and the next month I got my mortgage.

—Louise M., Boise, Idaho

applying for a mortgage

Let lenders and brokers shoulder the burden

There are two philosophies on applying for mortgages. Traditional conventional wisdom states that you should treat it just like any other professional relationship: Find a local partner you trust, and work to get the best deal and lowest rates from them.

Increasingly, however, many home buyers put in multiple applications for a mortgage, then check to see which lender will approve them for the lowest interest rate and fees. Lenders from across the country may now compete against one another for business.

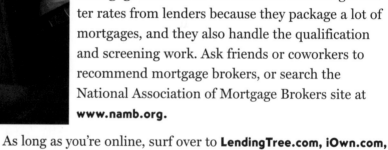

If you want to shop around, you have two options: **mortgage brokers** or the Internet. Brokers get better rates from lenders because they package a lot of mortgages, and they also handle the qualification and screening work. Ask friends or coworkers to recommend mortgage brokers, or search the National Association of Mortgage Brokers site at **www.namb.org.**

As long as you're online, surf over to **LendingTree.com, iOwn.com,** or **Priceline.com.** Through these and other Internet services, you can actually fill in a form and receive competing bids from multiple lenders. You can generally complete the formal mortgage application online as well.

If you don't feel like filling out forms, check out **Bankrate.com** to search for competitive loans in your area.

Keep in mind that putting in two formal applications for a mortgage will double your application fees, which are typically around $300.

ASK THE EXPERTS

Why shouldn't I just go to my local bank for a mortgage?

You can, but don't be afraid to shop around for the best rate. Once you've got an offer from a broker or online service, take it to your local bank and see if they'll match the offer. The worst they can say is no.

Should I ask lenders for an estimate of the closing costs they will charge?

By all means. Lenders are required to give you a good-faith estimate of closing costs. The amount varies widely from lender to lender, but a good rule of thumb is that closing costs will be 2% to 3% of the cost of the house. Lenders have been known to charge for everything from the fee for the lender's attorney and assessor to the copying costs for the required paperwork. Keep a sharp eye on these expenses as you weigh various offers.

What are "points," and should I pay them?

To a lender, a point is a percentage of the mortgage that you pay entirely up front. Generally, the more **points** you can afford, the lower the rate a lender will be willing to give you. If you plan on staying in your home for a long time, sometimes it makes sense to "buy down" the interest rate you'll have by paying points up front. If you do, make sure your accountant knows that you are doing so, because points are deductible when you're buying a home.

homeowner's insurance

You've gotta have it

Lenders are pretty conservative people. Case in point: Your lender will demand that you carry homeowner's insurance on your house before closing your mortgage. This is nonnegotiable. A fire could destroy your home, which would also destroy the lender's collateral, so the lenders want to protect their business interests.

They are not, however, protecting yours. (Well, not completely.) The lender will insist only that you get a bare-minimum policy. It's up to you to decide whether you'd like more protection. With as many options as a new car, homeowner's insurance can be bewildering. According to the National Association of Insurance Commissioners, the average cost of a homeowner's policy for a median-priced U.S. home in 1999 (the most recent data available) was $346 per year. As a general rule, more insurance (such as coverage for a more expensive house) equals higher costs, but you can reduce your monthly payments by going with a higher **deductible**—the amount you pay out of pocket before the policy kicks in.

Homeowner's policies are divided into broad categories. The most basic (known as **HO-1**) is what the lenders demand. In addition to your house, it also covers some personal property. It does not cover damage from falling objects, a heavy snowpack on your roof, or electrical surges, which require a more extensive package. Different basic grades cover almost every possible physical calamity, except for floods, hurricanes, and earthquakes.

Natural disasters aren't the only risk to your house. Should someone slip on your icy walks, you could be subject to a lawsuit. Basic policies' liability protection might seem substantial (say, $100,000) until you consider the $1 million payouts many juries have awarded in recent years.

ASK THE EXPERTS

What should I do if my house is at risk for a hurricane, earthquake, or flood?

Buy special insurance, which your lender will likely require. Florida insurance brokers offer special hurricane insurance, just as California brokers sell earthquake coverage. With the increasing costs of natural disasters in those two states, however, premiums and deductibles are rising. The same with flood insurance in several Midwestern states—until the Federal Emergency Management Agency had to step in to provide insurance at affordable rates.

What can I do to keep my insurance costs down?

Some of the basics include adding fire alarms and extinguishers, dead bolts for the front door, and a burglar alarm. Ask your insurance broker for a complete list of discounts and add as many security enhancements as makes sense.

Am I covered for the theft of family jewelry?

Valuable items like jewelry and computers are not covered by basic policies. Make sure to add a rider—insurance for specific items such as jewelry—which typically costs a fraction of your overall policy.

My basic policy's liability coverage seems low. Can I boost it?

Absolutely. You can broaden your personal liability coverage through an **umbrella policy,** which can cover large jury awards in civil court. They do not, however, protect your home from business judgments against sole proprietors.

Panic Attack

Great. In order to close on the house, I need to get homeowner's insurance. But the insurance company needs to know how many circuit breakers there are in the new house. What?! I have to go count them? Maybe it's in the inspector's report? If not, I need to make time to track down the agent, who has the key and who can let me in—again.

closing day

Clinching the deal

They say that the waiting is the hardest part, but it's not quite true. After signing the contract, putting money in escrow, and having the house inspected, you may find yourself waiting weeks to have your mortgage approved. Then one day you'll receive a commitment letter from the lender, stating that they have approved your loan.

Suddenly, you'll be thrown headfirst into the complicated, crucial closing phase—the process of completing all the details of the purchase. Closing will be like a whirlwind reunion of everyone you've worked with so far as you make sure all the inspector's concerns have been addressed, all the lawyer's questions have been answered, and all the money has been squared away. Refer to the following timeline to make sure you don't miss anything.

When you receive the commitment letter:

- Fax or mail the commitment letter to your attorney. She will have received a closing statement from the seller's attorney identifying various payments and credits, including incidental expenses.

- If it's not already in the contract, coordinate a closing date and location with the lender's closing agent or attorney.

- Ask your employer for a vacation day on the closing date. Having the time off will ease your mind if the closing runs later than you expect.

A week before closing:

- Give yourself a week to transfer funds from a money market or other account before asking your lender to cut a cashier's check.

- Ask your attorney to prepare a comprehensive list of everything you need to bring to the closing. This will include specific information about the checks you will write, including the check recipient's (seller's) proper name, the type of payment, and the amount.

The day before closing:

- Review the commitment letter, which lists several items that the lender expects you to bring to the closing. These can include cashier's or certified checks for specific amounts (personal checks will work only for small amounts).

- Remind your attorney to confirm the title insurance company's presence at the closing, in case questions about liens arise (see page 54).

- Conduct a final walk-through of the house on the day before or the morning of the closing. Verify that the seller has done everything requested in the contract: for example, pulled up old carpets, swept the house, and left in place any furnishings that were part of the sale. If you have a real estate agent, it's helpful to have her walk

through the house with you to act as a witness to any problems.

Closing day:

■ This is moot for people who live in states that let homeowners close using notarized mail. For states that require face time, don't forget to bring the signed contract and a photo ID, as well as proof that you've bought insurance for the new home.

■ Be prepared to sign multiple documents—including the lender's note, the mortgage, and acknowledgment that the lender has explained its fee procedures. Your arm may feel like it's about to fall off. But at the end of the day, you'll walk out as the owner of a new house.

■ More than likely, the closing will take place in a conference room in one of three spots: a lawyer's office, a bank's attorney's office, or an escrow company. A big conference table is usually necessary, because a lot of people will attend, including you, the seller, your attorney, the seller's attorney, the bank's representative, and the real estate agent (or agents, if you were shown the property by one who didn't represent the seller). This number can swell dramatically with specialists like a settlement agent or title insurance broker added in. Occasionally, but rarely, the seller is not there because he has assigned his attorney to work on his behalf. The presence of so many people should help ease any of your remaining anxiety. They've got as much at stake in this deal as you do.

■ Depending on where you live, there may be numerous other documents to sign, such as letters of agreement from lenders, and various tax papers. Make sure that your attorney explains everything to you. If you've got questions about anything, ask her. If it hasn't been paid in full already, you'll hand over the certified check paying the balance of your down payment. Loan fees are generally bundled into the amount of your mortgage, so you've paid them by signing the mortgage note. (Don't forget to give your accountant a copy of your closing statement—it might have information that's relevant for preparing your taxes.)

■ Finally, the seller hands over the house keys and that's it. You're a homeowner! Shake hands, say goodbye, and go celebrate.

the closing process

Stay on top of paperwork and deadlines

Congratulations! You've found the house you want, and your bid has been accepted. Your next challenge: You need to apply for a mortgage, convince the lender that you're creditworthy, and then address all the outstanding questions you, the seller, and either of your attorneys have before the closing date.

Welcome to the wonderful world of paperwork. Get ready to make plenty of copies and send overnight packages all over the place. Here's what to expect in the homestretch.

Before you apply for a mortgage:
- Check your credit record with the ratings agencies.
- Cancel any unnecessary credit cards.
- Correct any inaccuracies on your credit record.
- Research mortgages online or through a mortgage broker to find the best deal possible. Compare interest rates and fees.
- Consider whether you want to pay extra up front (points) to get a lower rate.
- Make a decision about whether to go with a fixed- or adjustable-rate mortgage.
- Fill out a mortgage application and collect everything that it requires, including bank statements and tax returns.

Once you've submitted your mortgage application:
- Call your lender the day after you drop off your application (or have it delivered) to confirm that everything was received by them.
- The bank will hire an appraiser, who will try to establish the home's value (which may be less or more than you're paying).
- Receive a commitment letter, in which the bank officially agrees to lend you the money and stipulates all the requirements you have to fulfill before closing.
- Lock in your mortgage rate so that it doesn't rise before you close.

- Start collecting any additional information requested in the commitment letter and send it to the lender.

- Obtain title insurance (your attorney will arrange this) to make sure that the seller has the right to sell you the property and that it is free from any legal or financial claims against it.

- Call your lender regularly to confirm that she has received all the paperwork—for example, a property survey—demanded in the commitment letter.

- Once all the paperwork is complete and the lender says you can proceed to closing, start pushing for a closing date with the seller, both attorneys, and the lender, something the agents should already be doing.

Once you've got a closing date:

- The seller's attorney will send your lawyer a closing statement, which identifies payments and credits that affect the closing—such as the amount of heating oil in the house's tank.

- Ask your attorney for a list of all the checks and documents you need to bring to the closing.

- Get homeowner's insurance on the house and send proof of insurance to your lender (they'll insist on this).

- Set up your accounts for telephone, electric, oil, gas, cable TV, and so on to prevent any gap in service. Note: Most companies will not open an account for you until the seller has given them a shut-off date.

refinancing

You've just closed the mortgage. You're finally a homeowner. And the first thing you want to think about is refinancing? Believe it or not—yes—provided interest rates have lowered.

Refinancing is basically taking out a new mortgage to pay off the old one. You'll pay fees, go through an appraisal, and look into the possibility of paying **points.** (A point is 1% of the mortgage amount. If your mortgage amount is $200,000, a point will cost $2,000. A point refers to the loan amount, not the interest rate). In effect, it's like selling your house to yourself.

The advantage of refinancing is that you discount your mortgage, which reduces your monthly payment. Even with new fees for the loan, this can save you a bundle. You might even save enough money over the course of a 30-year loan to pay for your child's college tuition. The downside is that your loan term starts all over again. Refinance a 30-year mortgage after owning a home for five years and you'll probably get another 30-year mortgage.

Note: Some states levy a mortgage tax that is based on the amount of your loan. To avoid paying this a second time, talk to your new lender about refinancing your existing loan "**by assignment**." This will allow you to assign the unpaid balance of your first loan to the new lender and pay a mortgage tax only on any amount above the current unpaid balance.

Of course, you have to think carefully about this decision. Will you remain in this house long enough to make the refinancing worthwhile? Are you willing to pay points now for a lower mortgage?

ASK THE EXPERTS

How long does refinancing take?

It generally takes up to two months to finish all the paperwork.

Who can help me refinance my house?

You should look into the same sources that you checked out for your original mortgage, including the lender that holds your current mortgage. Mortgage brokers can be helpful here by bundling your application with those of several other homeowners to win discounts from lenders.

Doesn't a refinancing make sense only if there's at least a two-point difference in the interest rate?

That may be what your parents and other traditionalists tell you, but it doesn't reflect the current market. It's an old rule of thumb that no longer applies. Mortgages—including refinancing—are an incredibly competitive business these days. This competition has caused fees to come down dramatically. Reduced fees mean that you can frequently make money when interest rates are only one point (and sometimes even less) lower than your current mortgage. (If you buy points, you are not buying interest rate points. You are buying points off your mortgage amount. See page 94.)

Can I cash out equity in a refinancing?

Yes, you can. This is a particularly useful way of eliminating high-interest credit-card debt, buying a car, or making improvements to your house. Lenders, however, may charge you higher interest rates if you're taking equity out of your home.

now what do I do?

Answers to common questions

I'm still trying to figure out the monthly payment I can afford. How do I calculate my personal budget for after the sale?

You've collected all the data on your future home. Take your current budget and substitute the average utility cost of the house for your existing utilities. Replace your rent with your mortgage and taxes and add in the average cost of repairs, maintenance, and pest control. Then crunch the numbers.

How do I budget for the tax benefit that I'll be getting after buying a house?

The amount of your tax break depends on your tax bracket and your state tax laws. Ask your accountant to figure out the difference for you and then add this money back into your personal budget. He can help you fill in new W-2 forms with your employer so you immediately start seeing the extra income (from reduced taxes) in your weekly paycheck.

What if property taxes go up frequently in the area in which I'm house hunting?

You'd better take this into account. Pricey neighborhoods tend to have neighbors that are more willing to spend top dollar to educate their children—which leads to higher property taxes.

Rates were spiking just when we bought our new home. Since they've eased a bit, should we think about refinancing?

Because there are costs associated with refinancing, it depends on how far rates have dropped and how long you plan to stay in your home. A traditional rule of thumb used to be to refinance if you could reduce your rate two or more percentage points. Today, however, it could make sense with as little as a 1% drop, if you're planning on staying there a while.

Are there any factors besides interest rates that may affect my payments?

Yes, your local property or school taxes could rise. These taxes are usually escrowed with your mortgage lender, who pays them for you when they fall due. Some lenders let you pay them directly. If there is a rise in your local taxes due to a need to improve the schools or local municipal services, for example, your monthly payments will rise.

NOW WHERE DO I GO?!

CONTACTS

Experian
www.experian.com

Equifax
www.equifax.com

TransUnion
www.tuc.com

www.LendingTree.com

www.iOwn.com

www.Priceline.com

National Association of Mortgage Brokers
703-610-9009
www.namb.org

BOOKS

Keys to Mortgage Financing and Refinancing
By Jack P. Friedman and Jack C. Harris

All About Mortgages: Insider Tips for Financing and Refinancing Your Home
By Julie Good-Garton

All About Escrow and Real Estate Closings: Or How to Buy the Brooklyn Bridge and Have the Last Laugh!
By Sandy Gadow

Steiner's Complete How to Talk Mortgage Talk
By Clyde and Shari Steiner

Moving

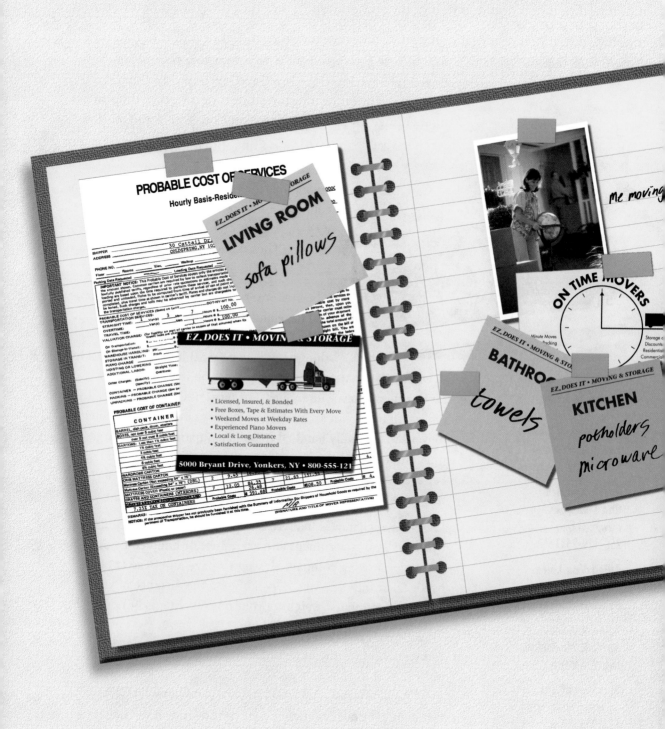

hiring movers

Give your back a break

You're racing toward closing. You're making phone calls to your lawyer, taking trips to the bank, and you're shocked that you've survived so far. In the midst of all this, you've got to think about another huge project: packing up your household and moving.

Top interstate van lines
(in order of size)

United Van Lines
www.unitedvan.com
636-343-3900

North American Van Lines
www.navl.com
260-429-2511

Allied Van Lines
www.alliedvan.com
800-470-2851

Atlas Van Lines
www.atlasvanlines.com
800-252-8885

Mayflower Transit
www.mayflower.com
636-305-4000

Enter the **professional moving company.** These firms will pack up your precious belongings for you and drive them across the country—or across town. Your goal is to get written price quotes from at least three movers. These should include both local and national companies.

The bids you receive depend on how much you have and how far you're moving it. Now is the time to sell, donate, or throw away things you haven't used for years. Keep a list of what you donate and get receipts. If you itemize on your taxes, this will save you money. For most new homeowners, the move will be within an hour or so of your current home. Such moves are generally handled by local companies who charge time and materials—say, three movers, times an estimated number of hours to pack and haul all your goods, times an hourly rate, plus the cost of boxes, tape, and packing materials.

Long-distance moves that cross state boundaries are regulated by the federal government and are generally handled by one of the major moving companies (see this page and page 113 for lists). Their bids will vary depending on the distance of your move, the estimated weight of your household goods, and such services as packing and unpacking.

Ask each firm for the names of several former customers. Find out whether any of their goods were damaged when moving. Ideally, you should start your hunt six to eight weeks before your move. Ask friends and family for referrals, check the yellow pages, or go online at **www.movingcenter.com.**

PROBABLE COST OF SERVICES

Hourly Basis-Residential

Certificate No.:

T-4168

ORDER NO. 0000000

DATE __00/00/00__

SHIPPER	SAMPLE	CONSIGNEE	SAMPLE
ADDRESS	COLDSPRING, NY 10516	ADDRESS	COLD SPRINGS, NY 10516
PHONE NO.		PHONE NO.	

Floor _____ Rooms _____ Elev. _____ Walkup _____   Floor _____ Rooms _____ Elev. _____ Walkup _____

Packing Date Requested _____ Loading Date Requested _____ Delivery Date or period of time requested _____

IMPORTANT NOTICE: This Probable Cost of Services covers only the articles and services listed. It is not a guarantee that the actual charges will not exceed the amount shown. Common carriers are required by law to collect transportation and other incidental charges computed on the basis of rates shown in the lawfully published tariffs, regardless of prior rate quotations or estimates made by the carrier or its agents. Exact charges for loading, transporting, and unloading are based upon the time required to perform these services, and such charges may not be determined prior to the time the goods are loaded, transported and unloaded. Rates to be computed from time of arrival of van at point of origin to the time the delivery and placing of shipment in new premises is completed, plus travel time as shown in carrier's tariff. Rates and charges do not include ferry, bridge or road tolls, or any other incidental charges which may be levied. Such charges and tolls may be advanced by carrier but are chargeable to the shipper or consignee. Charges for additional services will be added to the transportation charges.

PROBABLE COST OF SERVICES (Based on tariff _____ DOT-NY-MT No. _____)

PROBABLE CHARGES

TRANSPORTATION SERVICES:

STRAIGHT TIME: __1__ Van(s) __3__ Men __7__ Hours @ $ __100.00__ per hour $ __700.00__

OVERTIME: _____ Van(s) _____ Men _____ Hours @ $ _____ per hour

TRAVEL TIME: _____ __1__ Hours @ $ __100.00__ per hour   __100.00__

VALUATION CHARGE: (for liability on part of carrier in excess of that assumed when its lowest rates are charged)

On Transportation: $ _____ @ $.50 per $100, or fraction thereof   _____

On Storage-in-Transit: $ _____ @ $1.00 per $1000 for each 30 days or fraction thereof   _____

WAREHOUSE HANDLING: per _____ $ _____

STORAGE IN TRANSIT: From _____ To _____ @   _____

PIANO CHARGE   _____

HOISTING OR LOWERING _____

ADDITIONAL LABOR: Straight Time: _____ Men @ $ _____ per hour   _____

Overtime: _____ Men @ $ _____ per hour   _____

Other Charges: (Specify) _____

(Specify) _____

CONTAINER — PROBABLE CHARGE (See below)   __391.86__
__608.50__

PACKING — PROBABLE CHARGE (See below)   __608.50__

UNPACKING — PROBABLE CHARGE (See below)   __4.20__

TOTAL PROBABLE COST $__1,800.18__

If the total tariff charges for listed articles and services exceed the probable cost by more than 25 percent, then, upon your request, the carrier must relinquish possession of your shipment at delivery in advance of the payment of the total amount of charges shown on the bill of lading or freight bill. You are obligated to pay the balance of the total charges within 15 days.

Maximum amount to be paid at delivery of your C.O.D. shipment in cash, certified check or money order is (total probable cost plus 25 percent):

$ __N/A__

PROBABLE COST OF CONTAINERS, PACKING AND UNPACKING SERVICES

CONTAINER	CONTAINERS ☐ Loan ☐ Supply			PACKING			UNPACKING		
	Estimated Number	Per Each	TOTAL	Estimated Number	Per Each	TOTAL	Estimated Number	Per Each	TOT
BARREL, dish-pack, drum, etcetera	5	14.70	$ 73.50	5	23.60	$18.00			$
BOXES, not over 5 cubic feet									
over 5 not over 8 cubic feet									
CARTONS: Less than 1½ cubic feet									
1½ cubic feet	10	3.15	31.50	10	6.15	61.50			
3 cubic feet	15	4.45	66.75	15	9.55	143.25			
4½ cubic feet	8	5.50	44.00	8	11.65	93.20			
6 cubic feet									
6½ cubic feet									
WARDROBE CARTON	4	11.55	46.20	4	6.95	27.80			
CRIB MATTRESS CARTON									
Mattress Carton (Not exceeding 54" x 75")									
Mattress Carton (Exceeding 54" x 75") (DBL)	2	9.45	18.90	2	6.60	13.20	2	2.10	4.
MATTRESS COVER (Plastic or paper)									
CRATES AND CONTAINERS (MIRRORS)	7	12.05	84.35	7	21.65	151.55			
CONTAINER AND CONTAINER CONNECTOR			26.48						
7.25% TAX ON CONTAINERS	Probable Costs		$ 391.68	Probable Costs		$608.50	Probable Costs		$ 4.

REMARKS: _____

NOTICE: If the prospective shipper has not previously been furnished with the Summary of Information for Shippers of Household Goods as required by the Department of Transportation, he should be furnished it at this time.

__N/A__

(SIGNATURE AND TITLE OF MOVER REPRESENTATIVE)

do-it-yourself moving

Inexpensive but exhausting

More than likely, you're purchasing a home within an hour's drive of where you live now. That makes the prospect of a do-it-yourself move very tempting.

If you're determined to go it alone, give yourself enough time to organize your belongings. Moving will take twice as long as whatever you imagine.

Doing it yourself is never easy, but it may be easier if you live in a very small house or one-bedroom apartment.

Try to schedule the closing for your new home a week or more before the new occupants take over your old home or, if you rent, before your lease is up. You can move the bulk of your furniture with an appropriately sized rental truck in one day. After that, ferry over extra items— as well as clean up the old place—at a more leisurely pace. Moving most of your home in one trip will save time and, possibly, money.

Don't expect a do-it-yourself move to be cost-free, however. You'll need to rent a truck from a company like U-haul (**www.uhaul.com**) or Ryder (**www.yellowtruck.com**). (Even if you own an SUV, it won't hold that much furniture.) You'll also need to buy boxes, padding, and packaging tape. You can get these supplies and others from truck-rental firms, self-storage facilities, or even online, at **Allboxes.com.**

You may want to hire professional movers to pack original art, china, other fragile valuables, and to move superheavy pieces of furniture.

Most truck-rental firms offer cargo insurance to protect your goods. Although capped at a $25,000 total value, this provides some coverage when moving your possessions yourself. Renter's or homeowner's policies will not cover goods damaged in transit during a move.

ASK THE EXPERTS

Is there anything I can do to make my move easier?

Physically, yes: Stretch before and after the move, as if you're going to have a complete workout at your gym. Even if you do stretch, expect to ache for a few days afterward.

Don't pack a box so full that you can't lift it. Use small boxes for heavy items such as CDs or books; pack light items such as pillows in larger boxes. Wrap fragile items with newspaper or packing paper, surround them with plenty of Styrofoam packing nuts or wadded paper, and clearly mark the boxes as fragile.

How can I spare myself some of the aches and pains?

Pick up boxes the proper way. Squat down instead of bending at the waist. Use dollys and hand trucks.

What are the hidden costs of moving myself?

Many people forget to include the costs of fuel and mileage when renting a truck. Ask the rental company for the average miles per gallon of a fully loaded truck and its mileage rates over any daily allowance. Also, look for drop-off fees if you won't be returning the vehicle to the original location. Add in the cost of poorly packed, broken fragile items if you don't purchase insurance to cover your belongings during a move. Finally, there may be health costs: Temporary aches will gradually heal. But be careful about aggravating old back injuries or creating new ones.

Moving to a new city

- Decide how to move your car or else sell it and buy a new one when you arrive in your new city.

- Make hotel reservations or other arrangements for where you'll sleep after the bed is packed.

- Close your checking account— after you open one in your new town and you're sure that there are no outstanding checks pending against the old account.

- Notify your auto insurer of your new city.

- Pack the coffeepot, coffee, tea, bath towels, scissors for unpacking, and other essentials in the last box loaded on the truck so it is the first to come out.

- Keep important papers with you and away from the movers, such as airline tickets, marriage certificate, wills, and birth certificates.

- Keep moving receipts. You can deduct the cost of a job-related move.

- Arrange travel. Use frequent-flyer miles or coupons.

- Get medical records from your doctors.

packing

Getting your goods together

Packing and unpacking make up the bulk of the work in a move. Leave yourself more than enough time. Keep in mind how you'll want to unpack in your new home when you are organizing and packing. That way, moving in will be as easy as moving out.

Plan on it taking twice as long as you think it will to pack or to organize your things for the movers to pack. Just the same, plan on the movers taking half as much time to remove your things. They're fast, and they'll pack anything in their path not marked "Don't move." If you haven't emptied the trash before the movers arrive, you'll likely find it in a box in your new home.

To begin with, don't pack what you don't need. Isolate the worn couch, never-used wedding gifts, and other things you don't want. Have a yard sale or donate them to charity. Whatever charities refuse, take to the dump.

As you pack, mark each box by room and number it. (Consider color-coding the boxes.) You should create an inventory of what went into each box. If you're hiring someone to pack, they'll provide an inventory as well—but only of which box came from which room. Take your own notes as they pack; it'll save you hours of frustration after you move in.

Pack a clearly labeled **emergency box** or two. This should contain essentials for after you've moved in. Think of it as carry-on luggage, which can see you through any initial emergencies. Include daily necessities such as bedsheets, toiletries, towels, and basic eating utensils, including paper plates.

Finally, make sure you haven't accidentally packed tools you'll need to unpack, such as a pocketknife, hammer, screwdriver, flashlight, or tape measure. Likewise, if you hire movers, place birth certificates, wills, wedding certificates, and other important papers in a suitcase or file marked "Do not move" that you keep with you.

ASK THE EXPERTS

Can I save money by packing boxes myself, instead of having the moving company do it?

Movers charge a fee for each box they pack and a fee for the packing material. One way to cut costs is to do the packing yourself, except perhaps for expensive items like fine china. Another way to save a bit of money is to buy the packing materials yourself and leave the packing to the movers. However, most moving companies will not accept liability for boxes with your packing material unless you purchase additional insurance coverage.

Are newspapers good for packing fragile items?

Old newspapers make an inexpensive way to insulate your fragile goods. They create a mess, however, because newsprint readily bleeds ink. If you can afford it, pick up an ample supply of packing paper, which looks like blank newspaper, when you get your moving supplies.

FIRST PERSON DISASTER STORY

LET THEM DO IT

The dining room was empty except for the fine china on the floor. I brought the VCR, file cabinet, office supplies, art, pillows, blankets, and other stuff here, making a central packing area, hoping it would save the movers time and cut my labor costs. I realized, to my chagrin, that there was no room for boxes. Any false move would break everything fragile! The packers deftly worked around both obstacles. But the real headache started in our new home when I tried to find pillows, towels, anything! Every box was marked "dining room." Next time, I'll leave items where they belong and use my time making inventory lists. **—Georgia F., Los Angeles, California**

unpacking

Welcome to your new home

The day your movers arrive at your new house will be a blur. Your furniture will be flying off the truck, and boxes will be piling up in the empty rooms. Relax: This is the fun part. You now own the house and you're about to put your own decorating stamp on it.

Take a few steps to ensure that the next few weeks go smoothly—because it may take that long or longer to unpack all your stuff.

Unpack any carpets first, so you don't have to lift up furniture later. After that's done, set up your bed so you have a place to sleep tonight.

Organize the bathroom next. This will help you resume a normal routine with a shower as soon as that night or the next morning.

Next, tackle your kitchen. Aside from saving you money and bringing you closer to eating breakfast, cooking will make your new house seem more like home. From there, unpacking is a matter of personal taste and necessity.

Easing the move for children

Pack your children's rooms last. Children older than 5 can help pack. Let them write their names on their boxes. Give them time to talk about moving, their fears, and leaving friends behind.

After the move, set up the children's rooms first. It will have been a long day and they're likely to be exhausted. Plus, you all will be happier if they are safely playing in their room, out of harm's—and the movers'—way. Arrange for a familiar face as a sitter. As soon as you can, place your children's artwork on the refrigerator. Most important: Listen, especially after their first day at a new school.

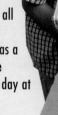

ASK THE EXPERTS

My coffee table looked great coming off the truck, but had scratches by the time the movers put it in the living room. Do I have any recourse?

Check the inventory list. Professional drivers and movers will acknowledge and indicate on it any damage they caused. If not, you get to note damages made when the list is presented to you for your signature. Use the moving company's insurance form to file a claim.

How do I file a claim?

When the movers pack up your goods, they'll create an inventory that details preexisting imperfections, such as a chipped dresser. You need to sign the inventory to officially agree with its assessment that it accurately includes everything. After the move, use this inventory list to check for missing boxes or furniture. Find out the deadline for filing any claim. If you find any damages among boxed items, leave the item in the box. (The movers may want to inspect the box's condition.) Use the mover's claim form to file a claim, attach copies of any sales receipts, and get ready to rumble. Call the mover every 30 days to hasten your settlement.

Boxes I left at the curb a week ago for collection are still there. What do I do?

Double-check your new community's trash and recycling schedule. Unpacking creates a lot of trash, and some communities limit the amount of waste you can place on the curb at one time. You also need to know whether you have to break down and bundle cardboard boxes for recycling.

Panic Attack

Mom will be here right after we move, but the couch and guest bed won't be delivered yet. Uh-oh! No place for her to sleep! Reality check: I'll buy a bed-in-a-bag, or rent a hotel room. Or give her my bed and sleep on blankets on the floor. She's coming to see me, not the new bed.

pets

Special care for special friends

Moving living creatures takes a bit more work than moving furniture. Pets don't like being packed up, and they don't like seeing their surroundings packed up around them.

In the days before the move, take your pets to a friend's house or board them at an animal hospital. This keeps them out of the mess and reduces the stress that may result from changing their surroundings. Vets that offer boarding are a particularly good option—combine the stay with a physical and stock up on any medications when you pick up your pet.

If you're moving more than half an hour's drive from your current home, however, you'll need to find your pet a new veterinarian. Ask your current vet for a recommendation or visit the American Animal Hospital Association Web site at **www.healthypet.com/mailtool/index.html.** Ask the new vet whether there are any restrictions on pets in your new community, such as registering your dog. Give yourself at least two weeks to finish up any required paperwork.

Despite your best efforts, pets sometimes run away from their new homes. Make sure your pet has an ID tag on its collar with your new phone number and address. Stash a picture and written description of your pet in your emergency box, just in case (see the section on packing an emergency box on page 104). That way, you'll have the material to make a missing-pet poster.

FRAGILE

plants

Bringing them along

Plants require their own care. The schedule below explains the steps to take to move your plants. If you're a dedicated gardener, you shouldn't let the movers take your plants along; the stress of traveling in a hot truck can kill the hardiest of plants. If you're moving nearby within the same day, you can take your plants in your car. Protect them by placing them in a packing box secured at the base with wadded-up paper. If you're moving to a new city and a new climate, you would be wise to take only the toughest of your container plants. Decide what plants will survive and what to give away. Figure out a way to drive them to your new location.

Three weeks before moving day Repot your plants from clay or porcelain containers into unbreakable plastic ones. This gives them a chance to adapt to new planters and lets you safely pack their fragile receptacles.

Two weeks before Prune your plants. This reduces their size for moving and decreases the chance of breaking branches haphazardly.

One week before Kill bugs on the plants by putting plants in a black plastic garbage bag for six hours with a pest strip or an animal flea collar. Keep the bag in a cool, shady area.

Two days before Water the plants as you would normally.

The night before Box the plants and set them aside so that the movers don't touch them.

Day of the move Move the plants yourself and unpack them in the new house as soon as possible.

creating a schedule

A good move takes lots of planning

Whether you do it yourself or hire professionals, moving a household can be daunting. You're still recovering from finding the perfect place and completing the vital details of its purchase. Now comes a project that can easily take two months.

Breathe! Like driving with directions, moving with a plan eliminates most headaches. So create a schedule, and stick to it.

Two months before the move		One month before

- Decide if you will hire movers or do it yourself.

- Ask friends, family, and colleagues to recommend moving companies and offer any advice.

- Call movers for price quotes and references.

- Decide what's going to the new house before the moving estimator arrives.

- Submit a change-of-address card to the post office or fill it out online.

- Notify everyone of your move: family, friends, your employer, colleagues, bank, insurance company, utility companies, credit-card companies, and doctors.

- Contact your insurance company to see whether your goods will be covered during your move. Get additional insurance from the mover accordingly.

- Select a moving company or reserve your rental truck if you're going to move yourself.

- Arrange for gas and/or electric service to start at your new location the day before you move in and to cut off service at your current home one day after you move out.

- Hold a garage sale for any items you don't want to move or donate them to a local charity.

FOR SALE

Your first stop should be the local post office to get the United States Postal Service's (USPS) free moving packet. It includes change of address forms, coupons, and, best of all, a convenient schedule that will help you plan most aspects of your move.

You can also file your change of address online, print out the forms, create a personalized moving timeline, and find more tips at the postal service's **MoversGuide.com** Web site.

Two weeks before	One week before	One day before
■ Transfer prescriptions to a pharmacy closer to your new home. Just in case, make sure you have an adequate supply.	■ Confirm arrangements with the moving company or truck-rental firm.	■ Get extra cash from the ATM for tips for the movers and to pay for other items.
■ Return any borrowed library books or neighbors' baking dishes. Reclaim any items you've loaned that you'll want to keep.	■ Take down any curtains, shelves, or other removable items that you want to take to your new home. Start cleaning bathrooms and the kitchen.	■ Get a good night's sleep.

Moving day

Two weeks before	One week before	Moving day
■ Start packing. If you're moving yourself, make sure to line up any help from family and friends.	■ Double-check the attic or other storage places for items you may have forgotten.	■ Walk through your current home after it's empty to make sure you didn't forget anything.
■ Arrange to donate unsold garage sale items to a local charity.	■ If you rent, ask your landlord to list any needed repairs so you can get your security deposit back.	■ Do a final cleaning of the house.
		■ Turn off all the lights and appliances.
		■ Leave your new address and phone number with a neighbor in case of emergency.

Based on the USPS guide, with a few alterations.

now what do I do?
Answers to common questions

I have to move out of my current house several weeks before I can move into the new one. What should I do?

Ask whether the previous owners of your new house can store your household goods temporarily. Your moving company may provide low-cost, short-term storage. If not, rent a storage facility for a month and plan on two moves. You might live with family or friends, or rent a short-term furnished hotel room that charges by the week or month.

I'll be exhausted at the end of the move. Do I really need to clean my old apartment?

It's tempting to leave it dirty, but getting lazy now could cost you money if your landlord takes the cleaning money out of your deposit. Why not hire a professional cleaner for a fraction of that amount and recoup some of your deposit—while saving your strength?

Should you tip movers?

Yes. If a team of people is moving your goods, you tip the driver, who then disburses the money to the team members. Each person should get anywhere from $10 to $20 each. Why the extra cash outlay? Think of it as extra insurance: For local moves, this same crew will likely be unpacking you. Friends also need a tip, so treat them to dinner after you're done—even if it's pizza and beer among the boxes in your dining room.

What should I do about appliances that I'm taking with me?

Look in your owner's manual, which should tell you whether any special care is needed to move them. Washing machines, for instance, need to be drained of any water. You also may have to remove loose items like revolving glass plates from a microwave.

Is it normal for a mover's bid to include extra charges for stairs?

Generally movers will charge extra only if they have to walk up more than two flights of stairs. These charges vary by mover and are a good reason to compare multiple bids.

Should my mover be insured and bonded?

Definitely. Insurance guarantees that you'll receive some compensation in case your goods are damaged in transit. Generally, these policies cover very little. Make sure you ask about the terms of the company's insurance. Often they'll sell you more coverage at a fairly minimal cost. Check to see if coverage is for full cost or depreciated value—the difference between collecting the actual $1,200 you paid for that big-screen television two years ago or only perhaps $600. Decide if you want a deductible, which brings down the cost of insurance. **Bonding** means that the mover has placed money with either a government agency or a bonding company to cover any potential penalties it might incur for not following regulations. It's a good sign, and it shows that the firm is a serious business operation.

NOW WHERE DO I GO?!

CONTACTS

United States Postal Service
(moving advice)
www.moversguide.com

National Moving Network
(a discounter for long-distance moves)
800-722-9775
www.nationalmoving.net

United Van Lines
636-343-3900
www.unitedvan.com

North American Van Lines
260-429-2511
www.navl.com

Allied Van Lines
800-470-2851
www.alliedvan.com

Atlas Van Lines
800-252-8885
www.atlasvanlines.com

Mayflower Transit
636-305-4000
www.mayflower.com

U-haul
www.uhaul.com

Ryder
www.yellowtruck.com

Packing supplies
www.allboxes.com

BOOKS

Smooth Moves
By Ellen Carlisle

Smart Moves: Your Guide Through the Emotional Maze of Relocation
By Nadia Jensen

Goodbye, House: A Kids' Guide to Moving
By Ann Banks

Improvements/ remodeling

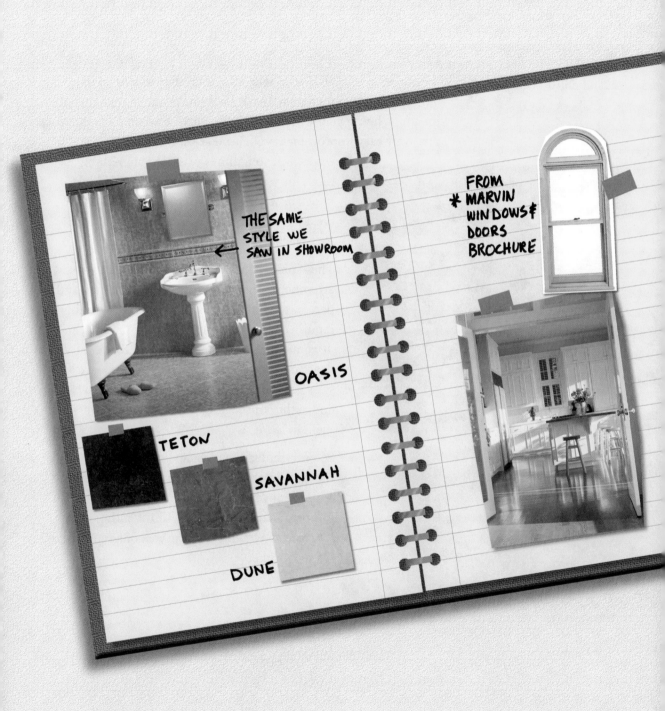

timing

Improvements may be easier before moving in

Most people start putting their imprint on a house as soon as they take ownership. Bookshelves and lighting fixtures go up; old wallpaper comes down. These are some of the ingredients of making a house your own. Sometimes you can accomplish these relatively easy improvements while you're still unpacking the boxes. But sometimes you want something more for your new house. Maybe you'd like to knock down the top half of a kitchen wall to create a breakfast counter. Perhaps you want to replace the bathroom's 1960's-era pink tiles.

These projects require more than a Saturday afternoon—and significantly more money. And here lies a dilemma: Major projects invariably require drilling, sawing, installing drywall, and disconnecting plumbing. Then there are the dust and chemical smells. All this can leave your new home in a mess. And you'll have to dodge the construction workers, who never seem to leave.

So even though you just spent months hunting for your dream house, if you are going to do major renovations, consider waiting to move in. Just make sure you can afford both the mortgage payments and the cost of a rental in the meantime.

ASK THE EXPERTS

I can't afford to rent while workers remodel my house. What can I do to reduce the inconvenience?

If it's at all possible, segment your house. Force the construction crews to use a different entrance than your guests. Put heavy construction paper on the floors to avoid scuffing. Place plastic over the door frames of the rooms being redone. If possible, use a hallway as a construction corridor, and use plastic sheeting to keep it separate from where you're living.

How can I control construction dust?

Drywall and joint-compound residue will get everywhere during construction, no matter how hard you try to control it. You can keep the dust buildup from getting out of hand with **high-efficiency particulate air (HEPA) filters.**

Will I need to get a permit to conduct the work?

That depends on your local laws. Call the building inspector as soon as you know how extensive your changes will be. Permits are typically required for major building, electrical, or plumbing work. Usually, your contractor applies for the permit. Part of the permit process requires the building inspector to check the contractor's work for any problems—such as using materials not up to code. You may have to submit plans to get a permit—a process that can further delay the start of your work (see "Permits," page 120).

How long will it take to do the work myself?

Many self-help guides—such as *Home Depot's 1-2-3* series—provide estimates for various projects. If you want to do the work yourself, read through several guides and plan on spending the maximum amount of estimated time on each project.

renovating costs

How much to spend and where to get it

Renovating your house can be expensive. It's also an investment: The value of your home increases with a newer kitchen or bath—usually not enough to offset the cost, but almost (see box below).

How can you pay for these improvements? You can always save for remodeling over time, and eventually pay cash for it from your savings. But if time is of the essence, it's good to know that money is available from lenders. Contact the bank that currently holds your mortgage and take out a **second mortgage** (which is just what it sounds like). It will run concurrently with your existing mortgage and require monthly payments. Or you can get a **home equity loan.** This loan has a shorter duration than a second mortgage, generally up to five years. You are allowed to draw up to a certain amount. What you draw on you pay interest—it's a bit like a low-interest credit card. (You must pay a minimum balance up to the due date.)

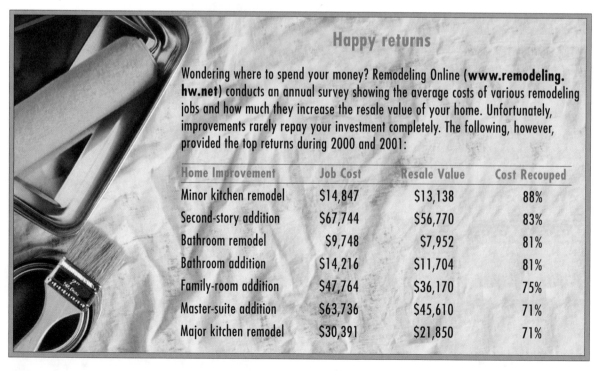

Happy returns

Wondering where to spend your money? Remodeling Online (**www.remodeling. hw.net**) conducts an annual survey showing the average costs of various remodeling jobs and how much they increase the resale value of your home. Unfortunately, improvements rarely repay your investment completely. The following, however, provided the top returns during 2000 and 2001:

Home Improvement	Job Cost	Resale Value	Cost Recouped
Minor kitchen remodel	$14,847	$13,138	88%
Second-story addition	$67,744	$56,770	83%
Bathroom remodel	$9,748	$7,952	81%
Bathroom addition	$14,216	$11,704	81%
Family-room addition	$47,764	$36,170	75%
Master-suite addition	$63,736	$45,610	71%
Major kitchen remodel	$30,391	$21,850	71%

ASK THE EXPERTS

How much should I spend on my renovation?

Plan on spending no more than 10% of your house's value for remodeling the kitchen. For bathrooms, the figure is 5% to 7%. Do your homework, and budget for your projects in advance. Any one of the hundreds of home-improvement books published each year will give rough estimates that can guide your budgeting.

If I don't have the money now, should I just wait?

Holding off for a year or two gives you a chance to determine how much you can really afford. You also will have time to learn things about the house that you never suspected at the outset. A major improvement that seems obvious a week before you move in might seem completely illogical a year or two later. Give yourself some time to discover how you actually live in the house. If that initial idea was a really great insight, it'll still make sense in another year. The difference is that you'll have had time to save the money to pay for it.

Can I put the costs on a credit card?

Yes, you can, but it's the most expensive way to go. At the very least, consider getting a store credit card from large housing-supply stores, such as Home Depot or Pier 1 Imports. First-time purchases usually come with a 10% discount.

permits

Play by the rules

Want to find out how your local government works? Just add a deck, wire the garage, or put a new bathroom in your house. Building codes and zoning ordinances rule most changes beyond the cosmetic. Local officials make and enforce these regulations.

The primary purpose of zoning laws is to separate business from residential areas—or dictate the balance between the two. However, they can also control other aspects of your proposed changes. They can limit how close to your property line you or anyone else can place any new structures. They can dictate the style of any changes to comply with a historic district's standards. Finally, they control environmental issues, such as building on a floodplain or encroaching on your house's septic tank.

Building inspectors (paid, appointed town officials) enforce the codes that provide basic standards for the technical aspects of a building. These include the foundation, plumbing, wiring, and fire safety. (The last item can include both the materials you use in your home and the house's design.)

To undertake major renovations, you have to secure a building permit. The inspector won't provide a permit without plans that detail the materials you'll be using. In a number of states, the inspector must also review the contractor's work in progress and upon completion. This is a very good thing, because the inspector can catch any potential problems and insist upon their correction.

ASK THE EXPERTS

Do I really need a building permit?

Don't try to remodel without a permit. Most towns allow building inspectors to levy fines for not having one. More importantly, you need an inspector to provide you with a **certificate of occupancy** (CO), the local government's seal of approval that the house is fit for habitation, when your project is done. Often, you can't get homeowner's insurance until you get a CO.

Can my neighbors make a fuss about my changes?

You bet. That's why it's always good to get them on your side. Show your neighbors your plans early in the process. If they have concerns, see if you can address them in your design. If they approve, ask them to write a letter to the governing authorities supporting your expansion. That vote of confidence will go a long way toward swaying reluctant board members (some towns have zoning boards that meet to review new housing and renovation projects).

architects and designers

An expert of your very own

Architects have a reputation for being expensive artistes who design grand buildings. In fact, most architects spend their days toiling away modifying existing structures and conforming homeowners' ideas to the hard realities of building codes. And relatively minor interior remodeling represents a significant part of their business.

Architects usually charge 8% to 15% of the total project's cost or else they charge by the hour at a specified hourly rate. In addition to ensuring that your changes comply with building codes, they act as a watchdog over contractors (see page 124). Architects shepherd your changes through the local government's permit process. They can also save you from making design mistakes that would reduce the value of your investment, such as neglecting the basic working triangle in your kitchen. (What's a working triangle? See page 130.)

A less costly alternative is to hire an interior designer. As long as your project doesn't include moving walls, plumbing, or wiring, an interior designer can help you choose materials and make design decisions.

If you're unsure of whether you need to use an architect or a designer, consider paying an architect for an hour's consultation. You can get a general idea of how much your project might cost, how large the fee might run, and how the architect will work. A consultation should cost no more than $100.

ASK THE EXPERTS

How can I find an architect or designer?

Friends and family are good sources for recommendations—especially those whose tastes are similar to your own. The American Institute of Architects (**www.aia.org**) and the American Society of Interior Designers (**www.asid.org**) also have search engines on their Web sites that allow you to find a member in your town.

What additional items will an architect charge me for?

Besides their fees, architects will generally charge you for travel to your site (although this may be negligible); printing and copying of documents, such as blueprints; postage; and any permit fees.

Can an interior designer handle structural changes?

Some can, some can't. Architects, however, have to pass exams that require structural understanding. Certain states won't provide a building permit without an architect's stamp on the blueprints.

Panic Attack

It's 3 a.m. and I'm still up worrying about the color of the tiles. Dove gray is too light; slate is too dark. I don't know. I kinda liked the peach. Heck, white is always safe. What's that saying? I know: If you don't know what you're doing, go for white.

contractors and tradespeople

Your construction supervisor

Prepare yourself. Architects' fees are modest compared with the cost of hiring a contractor or individual tradesperson, such as a carpenter or plumber. In some cases, labor represents 60% of the cost of a home improvement. There are ways to cut this down, but they all require that you do plenty of work yourself.

Tradespeople are specialists—among them are cabinetmakers, plumbers, and electricians. Contractors tend to be jacks-of-all-

trades. They're handy with carpentry, plumbing, and electrical wiring. They may bring in individual tradespeople to handle a particular chore, but they're competent enough to oversee an entire project.

The primary job of a **general contractor** is to manage the construction project. If you don't have an architect, the general contractor will handle getting the permits. You pay him in regular installments, and the general contractor in turn pays the individual craftspeople who work on your project.

ASK THE EXPERTS

How do I pay the contractor?

This should be spelled out in your contract. Depending on the size of the project, you may have to pay a portion up front and then make a final payment at the very end when all the work is completed to your satisfaction. For larger projects, you may pay in increments. Either way, be sure to withhold a sizable portion of the fee until you are satisfied that the work is finished.

Should the contractor have workers' compensation insurance?

Yes. Construction is a dangerous line of work. If your contractor doesn't have workers' compensation coverage, you could be on the receiving end of a lawsuit for workplace injuries that occur in your home. If a contractor says he doesn't need workers' comp, you should find another one.

Are there any qualifications for a contractor?

Yes. Make sure the contractor is licensed and bonded. Ask to see a license and insurance. You can find plenty of people who will offer to do the work without either, but licensing and insurance provide you with some protection against fraud.

How can I tell if I'm getting ripped off?

Get bids from multiple contractors. Ask them to detail their proposed fees and then compare them. Ask for references from recent customers. One reason to hire an architect is to help you identify potential scam artists and to hold the contractor to his contract once work begins.

dealing with contractors

Develop a payment schedule

So you've bought a home and now you want to remodel to create your dream house. You've decided you need a builder (also called a **contractor**) and/or an **architect** to do the work. There are important things to consider when drawing up contracts with these professionals.

If the work you're doing is aesthetic rather than structural (e.g., resurfacing the kitchen cabinets as opposed to building a new bathroom), you will probably just need to hire a contractor. If you're making structural changes, you may also need an architect. Before hiring anyone, ask to see examples of work they have done and get references. And when you interview former clients, don't be shy about asking whether the architect and contractor adhered to the budget and schedule, and whether their crews left behind a mess at the end of each working day.

You can also check up on construction professionals through the local Better Business Bureau or the Department of Consumer Affairs. Construction work often requires dealing with municipal boards and other local governing bodies, and you want to be confident that your team will be able to get the necessary permits and zoning approvals to do your project.

It's far from beginners' territory, but if you decide to raze the existing house and build a new one, you must enter into a construction agreement with the builder. Contracts for a home built to your specifications are very precise regarding materials to be used and other details.

Tips for dealing with contractors and architects

Once you've found the contractor and/or architect, here are some issues to consider:

Signing contracts Your contractor will want you to sign a contract that stipulates, among other things, the work to be done and the payment for it. If it's a big job, it's smart to have a real estate lawyer review it for you. A lawyer can make sure the contract protects you in case of default or poor performance by the contractor.

Developing a payment schedule Your contractor will want as much payment in advance as possible, but you'll want to delay payments to ensure that the contractor will do the work on schedule and finish the job. It's best to provide enough money up front to cover the contractor's building and materials expenses, but hold on to a major payment until the project is completed.

Inspecting the work Your architect can act as an inspector for what the contractor is doing (e.g., using the right materials, following the architectural plans). Some states require on-site inspections by your town's building inspector.

Obtaining permits Certain certificates of completion are issued by the local municipality after work is completed, and as the homeowner you will need to show all these certificates when you decide to sell your house. It's a good idea to tie the final payments to the receipt of all necessary certificates of approval.

Hiring subcontractors Make sure your contract states how subcontractors are to be paid. You'll also want to get releases (sometimes called **lien waivers**) from any subcontractors after they complete their work and you have paid the contractor. This will protect you from a subcontractor putting a **lien** on your house (a claim on a piece of property to secure payment for a debt) in the event that the contractor hasn't properly paid his subcontractors.

exterior improvements

Paint, windows, and bricks

First impressions matter. The quickest way to improve the look of your home from the outside is to paint it. However, before you buy the supplies, evaluate your home's exterior. The baked-in pigment of old aluminum or plastic siding may be fading, but you paint over it at your own risk. A new coat will not stick as well as the original layer, and it will eventually peel. Shingle and shake homes will likewise shed a layer of paint. (A **shake** is a shingle with one rough-hewn side, as opposed to a shingle's two sawed sides.)

Paint away, however, if your house has brick, stucco, or wood siding. Just keep in mind that painting your exterior is not a simple job. At a minimum, you'll need a ladder. Ideally, you should rent scaffolding, a power washer, and other tools to ensure you do the job properly.

Preparation is the key to a paint job's longevity. You don't want to repeat this chore frequently, so do it right. By scraping off all of the peeling paint and priming the surface, a latex paint will last about five years. An oil-based paint may last eight.

The basic rules for painting interiors and exteriors are the same. Start from the top and work your way down. Outdoors, the order goes: **soffits** (the underside of your roof's eaves), **fascia** (the board face of the eaves), siding, door and window trim, pillars or posts, and finally entry steps or porch. This ensures that paint doesn't splatter on your completed sections.

If you're scared of scaling heights or dedicating multiple weekends to painting, consider hiring a contractor for the job. As with all professionals, get at least three estimates and seek references from past customers. You'll learn how accurate the price quotes are—and whether you want to think again about doing the job yourself.

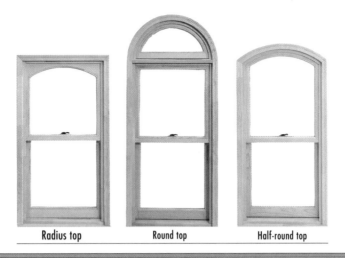

| Radius top | Round top | Half-round top |

Windows

Windows are an important architectural element of your home, but they're also a chief source of drafts. If your windows let in cold during the winter, they're also likely to let in heat during the summer. As a result, your heating and cooling bills will suffer. You can add storm windows or go through the tedious process of insulating your existing windows. Old windows may also have broken sash cords that prevent them from raising and lowering easily.

That's why many people replace windows. The improved energy efficiency frequently recoups the investment over several years. New windows also can add style to your home and may be the only change you need to get the look you want. Styles include: radius top, round top, and half-round top. Manufacturers include Marvin (888-537-8268, **www.marvin.com**) and Pella (888-847-3552, **www.pella.com**).

Bricks

Tattered brick exteriors rarely look bad because of the bricks themselves. Most of the problem comes from the mortar that holds them together. If your mortar is crumbling, you should **repoint** your walls. (You'll also need to repoint the brick chimneys of wood-sided homes occasionally.) Repointing (also called tuckpointing in the Midwest) means chipping out the old mortar to the depth of about an inch and replacing it with new mortar.

Not all mortar is the same: It comes in different hues that can subtly change the look of your home. When trying out a new color mortar, test it around a section of wall. You can always chip out the sample if you don't like the look. For minor repairs, try to match the existing mortar color; otherwise your home will look like patchwork.

kitchen renovations

Cooking class

Many homeowners undertake a kitchen renovation at some point. But before you get carried away with grand visions of industrial-strength stovetops and walk-in refrigerators, remember that less-expensive minor remodeling jobs—which typically cost only half what a major one does—recoup more of their cost when you sell your home (see "Happy returns," page 118).

Follow the red dots to see a kitchen's working triangle.

Spackle and paint won't cover up fundamental flaws, however. Look at your kitchen. Draw imaginary lines between the stove, sink, and refrigerator. This is the **working triangle.** The three lines should total 12 to 24 feet, and there should be no obstructions between any two of these crucial points. You don't want to trip while taking vegetables from the refrigerator, washing them in the sink, and sautéing them on the stove.

Your triangle doesn't meet these standards? That's one reason to consider a more extensive kitchen redesign. If you're lucky, it'll just mean moving the refrigerator to a more convenient location and maybe adding an electrical outlet near its new spot.

More than likely, fixing a bad triangle means adding new cabinets. Such a renovation will usually entail hiring a plumber (to install the sink and dishwasher) and an electrician (to wire the garbage disposal and new outlets for moved appliances), which will be costly.

ASK THE EXPERTS

How long will a kitchen renovation take?

It depends on how extensive your renovations are. Doing the work yourself, you might finish a simple paint job and a new floor in a weekend. An extensive kitchen remodeling—including new cabinets, moving the sink, and installing new appliances— might take a couple of months.

Where do I cook while my kitchen's in disarray?

Not in the kitchen! Set up a temporary cooking space elsewhere in the house. Ideally, your provisional kitchen will be near a sink so you can clean dishes. Use your microwave oven a lot, or purchase a single electrical burner. Of course, there's always takeout.

Will I save money on electricity with new appliances?

If the existing appliances are only a couple of years old, probably not. They should be efficient enough so that you won't gain enough energy savings to pay for newer models. Holding on to existing appliances is also a way to knock down the cost of your kitchen renovation.

Isn't quality more important than price?

Be smart about where you save money. Avoid custom cabinets. Stores such as Home Depot and Ikea carry a range of attractive options that are reasonably priced. But fixtures are one place where you should spend the cash. A cheap faucet won't last as long as a quality one.

bathroom renovations

Fun with faucets

Bathroom renovations pay a fantastic return on your investment (see "Happy returns," page 118). They're smaller than any other room, less expensive to fix, and more functional than most. Bathrooms need your attention in three areas:

Floors and walls What you do here depends on how extensive your renovation will be. You can't install a new tile floor without pulling up your toilet and, possibly, your sink. You can, however, add a second layer of vinyl flooring over an existing one. Just don't go more than two layers deep. If you plan to rebuild a wall behind a shower or tub, make sure you use water-resistant drywall.

Vanities, showers, tubs, and toilets Bathroom upgrades get expensive when you start replacing these elements, but there are advantages. A new low-flow toilet can reduce your water usage and your ongoing monthly expenses. (Earlier versions from the 1990's frequently require a second flushing.) If you're adding a new tub or shower, now is a great time to add an anti-scald device—a requirement in most states' building codes for new construction.

Fixtures As with the kitchen, here is where you should spend money to get quality. Fixtures (such as faucets and lights) also help add distinction to an otherwise ordinary bathroom.

ASK THE EXPERTS

Where can I take a bath while my bathroom's being worked on?

The crucial question, in terms of planning, is how many baths your house has. If you plan to remodel your sole bathroom, however, you may need to camp out with friends or go on a vacation while the work is done. Got a half-bath (a toilet and sink) to fall back on? That plus your health club's shower can see you through the makeover.

How can I deal with strong or low water pressure?

The amount of water you use depends in part on your home's water pressure. Ask your plumber to gauge your pressure if your engineer didn't already include it in the inspection report. If it runs strong—say, 125 psi (pounds per square inch)—it's pushing water out faster than you need it. You'll probably want to buy a low-flow showerhead to reduce consumption. These typically limit the flow to 2.5 gallons per minute, compared with three times that rate for more wasteful nozzles. Anything less than 25 psi, however, will dictate your choice of toilets: You'll have to forgo pressure-assisted models—a more efficient, if more expensive, low-flow technology than gravity-assisted ones.

What's the best way to ventilate a bathroom?

Face it. Bathrooms get steamy, which can feel great in winter and yucky in summer. That steam can crack plaster and stain walls with mildew. Make sure that your remodeling includes adding a fan if one doesn't already exist. Check its capacity to make sure it can clear the steam within 15 minutes. If you're looking for a little extra warmth on cold days, ask your contractor about **radiant heat.** Whether provided by electrical means or by hot water, radiant heat warms up cold tiles. It's an indulgence that you'll appreciate for years to come.

adding a room

Spreading your wings

Whether it's for a new child or a new home business, sometimes you just need more space.

A new room can be simple or complicated. At its most basic, you can recycle an existing space in your house. You can finish a basement or attic. And an attached garage can become a new playroom or an apartment for an in-law—provided you're not violating any local zoning ordinances.

When adding to your house's exterior, the simplest construction is adding a second floor. Adding rooms on the ground level takes longer and requires pouring a new foundation and having it inspected—an expensive process. Approval is more complicated as well, since your house's footprint will be edging closer to the property line (see page 120).

In either case, you'll need to consult an architect about such extensive renovations.

Home sweet office

Adding a home office can be as easy as setting aside a corner of your living room. If you prefer not to see your pending paperwork when you're entertaining or relaxing, buy a decorative screen. If that's not enough or you want to avoid interruptions from family, designate a place where you can shut a door. Whether in the basement or in a spare bedroom, there are two things you'll need beyond a desk. First, make sure the room has a phone line. Most homes have four-wire telephone cabling that can be divided into two lines. Even if you don't add a second line right away, split the cable into two jacks. That will give you a separate line for a computer modem or fax machine when you need it. Second, check the room's electrical load—and that of the entire circuit—to make sure it can accommodate your computer, printer, scanner, and other electrical devices. Minor electrical interruptions can cause computer glitches, so add a surge protector as well.

FIRST PERSON DISASTER STORY

SUCH A NICE GUY

I knew to pay the contractors in installments, a little up front and then as the work progressed. And I knew to check references. But I was new in town and was anxious to get my kitchen renovated. I hired the least expensive contractor and didn't check his references. He was also the nicest. I should have known there was trouble the first day when he didn't show up at my house to start the renovation. But he called and apologized profusely, saying his truck had a problem. He showed up the next day and started ripping out cabinets and taking out the old sink. He was so cheerful; we chatted off and on throughout the week. He sort of felt like family after a while. After two weeks, he said he needed money for repair work on his truck or he wouldn't be able to come and finish the job. I gave it to him and told him it was a loan against future work. He never showed up again. I had no choice but to go after him in small claims court, only to find out that he had declared bankruptcy that month. There is a good reason why you check references and don't give out more money than is specified in the contract.

—Colleen S., Atlanta, Georgia

ASK THE EXPERTS

Will an addition or other major change to a house affect its taxes?

The folks who issue building permits generally let the assessor know that a building is undergoing a change. After you've completed construction, the assessor will visit to evaluate how much to increase the value of your home—and will raise your taxes accordingly.

What is a "punch list"?

As construction winds down, you'll find minor corrections or details that the contractor neglected. For example, maybe the hall is painted but the light fixture isn't installed yet. A **punch list** identifies all the items the contractor must finish before he receives final payment.

now what do I do?

Answers to common questions

Can't I do the work myself?

Have you ever repaired or constructed something in a home before? Do you prefer to work on your weekends rather than rest? Do you adjust easily when things don't work out as planned? Are you able to admit when you're in over your head? When you run into something you don't understand, do you research it? Can you handle local government red tape without blowing your stack? Are you ready for friends and family to ask repeatedly "when will it be finished?" If you can honestly answer yes to all these questions, you can consider doing many improvements yourself. Be sure to leave enough time to complete each one, and don't bite off more than you can chew.

Is there a way I can cut down on costs besides doing the work myself?

Yes. You can dispense with the general contractor and hire individual tradespeople directly. You act as the manager, scheduling everything and paying everyone. If you don't have an architect, you'll also have to get any permits yourself. This requires a thorough understanding of the project and a good grasp of construction before it begins.

Do I have to buy the supplies from a contractor or tradesperson?

You can buy the supplies yourself at stores like Home Depot or Lowe's. You can purchase fixtures online or by catalog. The only drawback is that you've got to arrange for their delivery. If you have sufficient storage space in your home, just order them in advance. If not, you'll need to coordinate deliveries for when they're wanted. A pickup truck, yours or a friend's, makes hauling the material around easier. Otherwise, you'll need someone at home to await the delivery. If you get your supplies from tradespeople, you should be sharing in their trade discount, which is anywhere from 10% to 40% retail.

How do I get rid of debris when I do the construction?

Don't plan on putting it at the curb. Depending on how extensive the work is, you may have to rent a Dumpster. Look in the yellow pages under "carting" for firms that rent Dumpsters and haul them away. For less extensive work, you can tie the debris up in heavy-duty bags, bring them to the local dump yourself, and pay a disposal fee. In any case, budget for trash removal.

Can I get some of my town's building regulations changed?

If what you want to do falls outside of the zoning or building codes, you will need to get a **variance** (an exemption from the code). The local zoning-board authority frequently agrees to variances in zoning regulations—but politics can affect your chances. So get political: Attend some meetings of the board to gain a sense of how they work (they're open to the public). Talk to its members—they may even be your neighbors. Ask them informally how amenable they are to a variance. More than likely they'll give you tips that will help get it passed.

NOW WHERE DO I GO?!

CONTACTS

Home Depot
770-433-8211
www.homedepot.com

Lowe's
800-445-6937
www.lowes.com

Remodeling Online magazine
www.remodeling.hw.net

National Association
of the Remodeling Industry
www.nari.org

www.handymanconnection.com/
(source of tradespeople in various parts
of the U.S. and Canada)

www.handymanclub.com
(members' only magazine for do-it-yourselfers)

Kohler Co.
800-456-4537
www.kohler.com

Marvin Windows and Doors
888-537-8268
www.marvin.com

The McGuire Furniture Company
800-662-4847

BOOKS

F. R. Walker's Remodeling Reference Book: A Guide for Accurate Remodeling Cost Estimates for Construction Professionals and Homeowners
By the Frank R. Walker Co.

The Kitchen Idea Book
By Joanne Kellar Bouknight

The Bathroom Idea Book
By Andrew Wormer

Additions: Your Guide to Planning and Remodeling
By Better Homes and Gardens

Landscaping

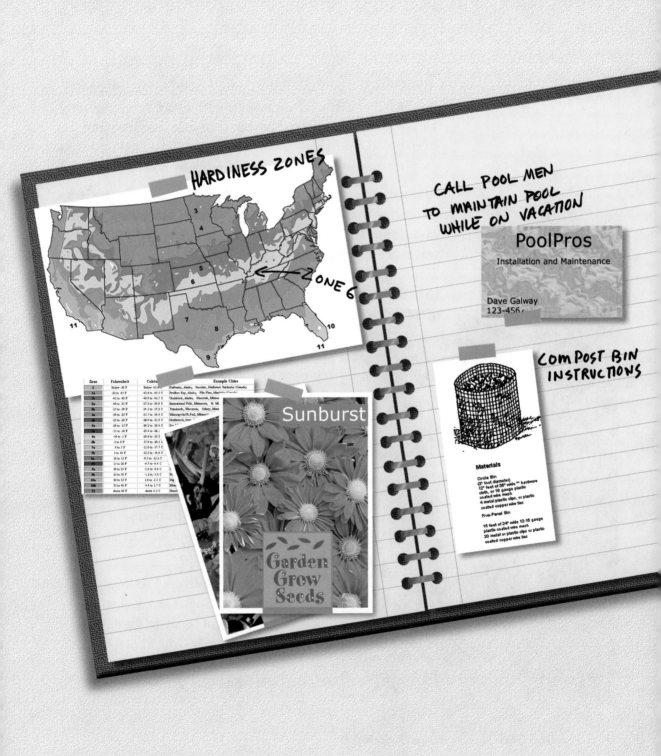

HARDINESS ZONES

4

5

6

ZONE 6

7

8

11

10

9

11

Zone	Fahrenheit	Celsius	Example Cities
1	Below -50 F	Below -45.6 C	Fairbanks, Alaska; Resolute, Northwest Territories (Canada)
2a	-50 to -45 F	-42.8 to -45.5 C	Prudhoe Bay, Alaska; Flin Flon, Manitoba (Canada)
2b	-45 to -40 F	-40.0 to -42.7 C	Unalakleet, Alaska; Pinecreek, Minnesota
3a	-40 to -35 F	-37.3 to -39.9 C	International Falls, Minnesota; St. Michael, Alaska
3b	-35 to -30 F	-34.5 to -37.2 C	Tomahawk, Wisconsin; Sidney, Montana
4a	-30 to -25 F	-31.7 to -34.4 C	Minneapolis/St. Paul, Minnesota
4b	-25 to -20 F	-28.9 to -31.6 C	Northwood, Iowa
5a	-20 to -15 F	-26.2 to -28.8 C	Des ...
5b	-15 to -10 F	-23.4 to -26.1 C	
6a	-10 to -5 F	-20.6 to -23.3 C	
6b	-5 to 0 F	-17.8 to -20.5 C	
7a	0 to 5 F	-15.0 to -17.7 C	
7b	5 to 10 F	-12.3 to -14.9 C	
8a	10 to 15 F	-9.5 to -12.2 C	
8b	15 to 20 F	-6.7 to -9.4 C	
9a	20 to 25 F	-3.9 to -6.6 C	
9b	25 to 30 F	-1.2 to -3.8 C	Big ...
10a	30 to 35 F	1.6 to -1.1 C	
10b	35 to 40 F	4.4 to 1.7 C	Mian ...
11	above 40 F	above 4.5 C	Honol ...

Sunburst

Garden
Grow
Seeds

CALL POOL MEN
TO MAINTAIN POOL
WHILE ON VACATION

PoolPros

Installation and Maintenance

Dave Galway
123-456...

COMPOST BIN
INSTRUCTIONS

Materials

Circle Bin
(3' foot diameter)
12" feet of 36" wide == hardware
cloth, or 18 gauge plastic
coated wire mesh
4 metal plastic clips, or plastic
coated copper wire ties

Five-Panel Bin

15 feet of 24" wide 12-16 gauge
plastic coated wire mesh
20 metal or plastic clips or plastic
coated copper wire ties

the grounds

The lay of the land

You're not just buying a house, you are also buying the land around it. For many, having a house with a yard is the main reason for leaving the city and buying a house in the great outdoors. Of course, the yard comes with a price: the more land—measured in acres—the higher your local property taxes will be.

So whether you relish the idea of a garden or couldn't care less, take a good look at the yard of your prospective house. Problems with shrubs and **perennials** (flowering plants that bloom every year) are pretty easy to see. Usually a little weeding, pruning, or fertilizing will bring them around. Not so with trees. If there are large trees, check to see if they have been pruned or **cabled**

(when thick wires are attached to the main limbs high up to prevent a limb from breaking off during a storm). Very large trees that are too close to a house may need to be cut down, at your expense. Droopy looking trees may require a call to an arborist to ensure that they don't have a disease. Elms, dogwoods, and California oaks are among the trees that are prone to problems. Because tree diseases can quickly spread, some local government agricultural services will inspect your trees for free. You, however, will have to pay for the removal of diseased trees.

Those who love to garden will see lots of potential. Those who don't love it should know that a well-kept lawn and garden can greatly enhance your enjoyment of the house—as well as increase its resale value when it comes time to sell.

ASK THE EXPERTS

I'm tempted to start fixing up the garden now. Is that a good idea?

Pruning, weeding, and fertilizing are always in order. But before you make any drastic changes, wait a year in order to see how the yard and garden fare in all four seasons. The unkempt shrub that you want to pull out in June may have beautiful berries in November.

When should I remove trees and shrubs?

If a tree is dead or diseased beyond saving, have it removed immediately. Large, dead branches that threaten your house should also get prompt attention. In arid areas of the West, many homeowners remove all trees and shrubs from within at least 30 feet of the house. This creates a firebreak that protects a home from wildfires. Do this before the dry season threatens your home. (Properties with **slope,** land that slants downward or upward, require even greater clearance—possibly more than 100 feet.) You'll need to landscape with rocks, flowers, and grasses instead.

What if I want to save a particular tree?

If you want to save a tree or shrub, you can move it. Fall and spring are generally the best times to move trees and shrubs, but in the Deep South you should avoid moving them in the spring. The plants will have too little time to acclimate to their new setting before summer's heat arrives.

lawns

Go for the green

Ah, the lawn. A good lawn acts like a beautiful frame around a painting. A quick walk across your yard should give you an idea of its quality. Are there more dandelions than grass? Several different types of grasses? You may have to rip up the lawn and start over. See any moss? That spot's not getting enough drainage, light, or fertilizer.

If you wish, you can also test your soil's **pH level** (its acidity and alkalinity) at a private lab. Plants will not thrive if the level is too high or too low. If you need to, you can adjust the pH to a plant-friendly level with lawn additives. Check with your local nursery to find out what additives are best used in your region.

If you'd like someone else to do all this yard work for you, hire a lawn service to handle it. Of course, you don't need a traditional lawn at all. Although some suburban subdivisions dictate lawns in their covenants, most homeowners are free to choose landscaping options. You can even plant your yard with decorative tall grasses, such as fountain grass or maiden grass.

ASK THE EXPERTS

How often should I mow, and how much?

Mow as often as it takes so that you're never cutting more than one-third the height of your grass at a time. Cutting grass when it is too long stresses a lawn. Local conditions will guide you. In some parts of the humid South, twice a week may work. During dry spells, growth slows and so can your mowing.

Does my lawn need a drainage system?

Check out your property's slope. If the incline runs away from your home, everything's fine. If not, that means rainwater may collect around your foundation or in your basement. Now is the ideal time to reslope your yard or insert a drainage system, before you invest in your lawn. The dirt you move may also require some support to hold it back, such as a retaining wall (see "Fences and Walls" on page 152).

How often should I water the lawn?

That depends on where you live, the weather, the time of year, and the type of grass you grow. A good rule is that a lawn requires about one inch of water per week. If it rains an inch, your lawn will be fine.

Panic Attack

I want to put stepping stones from the driveway to the house, but Hank is dead set against it. He says it will kill his lawn mower. Time for an Internet search. Ah! A **string trimmer** (a gasoline- or electric-powered tool that has a long handle like a rake and uses a material similar to heavy fishing line for cutting) cuts around any edge! Oh Haaaank . . .

gardens

Creating your own Eden

Great, you're in the house and it's been a year and you've seen the lawn and garden through the four seasons. And now you're itching to make some changes. Good for you. But what exactly should you do?

First, read up on plants and gardening. Then check that your choices will survive in local conditions. Two great local sources to consider: your gardening club and your nursery. As you plan, realize that adding a vegetable garden or flowerbed requires special siting. Vegetables require sun; flowers require water. Make sure that you've got a way to water any beds that you create. Double-check how large any existing trees will grow to be. That sweet little sapling near the patio will grow into a large water-guzzling maple in a few years' time. If you don't want it to take all the rainwater from your new perennial beds, it's best to remove it now.

Regardless of where you live, you'll want to conserve water, because its usage is frequently regulated and often metered. Consider gardening with so-called **xeriscape** principles, which seek to reduce water consumption through landscaping choices such as using extensive mulch, or planting with native species that are drought resistant.

ASK THE EXPERTS

What are "hardiness zones"? How do I tell which hardiness zone I'm in?

Palm trees can't survive northern winters. Peonies can't bloom without them. Botanists define **hardiness zones** to delineate which plants do well in a particular area. You need to learn which zone (numbered from 1 to 11) you live in and buy plants that will thrive there. Most gardening books—as well as several online sites—have maps to guide you. If your house appears to be close to the border of two regions, ask your local gardening club or nursery which zone best fits your location. Keep in mind that mountains and tall hills are colder than valleys, so you may be in a different zone from your neighbors down the hill.

I want to put in a garden, but I'm worried it will take too much time to care for. How much time is required?

That depends on what you've planted in the garden and how large it is. A good rule, however, is to spend 15 to 30 minutes each weekend doing basic tasks, such as weeding and watering. Once every other month, plan to spend a full day tackling larger tasks, such as pruning, fertilizing, or preparing for winter by cutting down withered stalks.

What is composting?

Composting is the natural process of converting leaves, grass clippings, pinched flower buds, and kitchen vegetable waste into a thick, coffeelike paste you can use to mulch or nourish your garden. Recycling your yard and kitchen waste will naturally improve the soil that your plants grow in. You can compost simply by throwing the material in a mound, though an unsightly heap may raise your neighbors' ire.

workspaces

Spots for potting

When you move in, it's natural to set up a work area in your kitchen or living room to serve as your home organizational center. The same goes for your yard. You need a place to accommodate your various outdoor pursuits—be it storing the lawn mower or bags of topsoil. Even if you just like puttering around the yard, it's still a good idea to plan a workstation. So think about adding, building, or renovating these spaces:

Toolshed A place to store your spades, rakes, and mower. Many people use a garage for this purpose. That's fine as long your tool collection doesn't get so extensive that it crowds out the car. If you've got an existing shed, it requires regular maintenance—including painting. Local zoning laws may regulate the placement of new ones, and etiquette dictates telling your neighbor before building a new one.

Planting station Patio tables are frequently used as the surface area for putting new plants in pots, but sitting (or stooping over) while you pot begonias will limit your productivity. Building a space where you can comfortably stand spares your back and speeds along your planting. If this station is placed in the yard, dirt will fall on the ground—lessening cleanup time.

Compost Don't throw away your yard waste. Composting turns all those clippings and scraps into the best plant food available. It takes four to six months for compost to be ready for garden use, however, so you should compost in a container, which is best placed out of sight but near an outdoor faucet for watering.

Yard Tools

Maintaining your yard requires certain basic tools. Here's a list of crucial accessories.

Wheelbarrow (**A**) An essential means of carting around heavy bags of topsoil, fertilizer, seed, and yard waste.

Weed whacker (**B**) A power trimmer that cuts grasses along borders where a mower can't reach.

Rake (**C**) For excess lawn debris and fall's annual leaf harvest.

Lawn mower (**D**) Unless the previous owner threw one in with the sale, you'll need to purchase a lawn mower. Make sure it fits your lawn: Large tracts require a riding mower; postage-stamp lawns might be better suited to a push-powered reel mower.

Sprinkler and hoses Droughts happen, even in the humid East. Make sure you've got sufficient length to reach from your external faucet to the far reaches of your yard.

Spreader A handy device that sows seeds and spreads fertilizer.

Edger Keeps the borders of your flowerbeds and the boundaries of your walks neat.

Spade General handy tool for reworking slopes, replacing sod, or moving shrubs.

decks and patios

Living in nature

Decks and patios are among the most common improvements that new owners add. That's because they're a fairly inexpensive way to extend the use of your house. A **deck** is a wood-floored outdoor space adjacent to your home. It can be on the same level as your home or several steps up or down. A **patio** is an outdoor space on the ground, generally paved with brick or stone.

New decks generally require the approval of a building inspector (see page 120), while patios may not. Existing decks need a careful inspection. Check under the deck for rotting wood. By replacing bad timbers you can enjoy your yard knowing that you're on secure footing. You'll also want to **seal** (paint with waterproof sealant) the deck against the elements.

Crumbling stone patios should also be repaired. It's easier if your patio has been built on a sand foundation, but you can still chisel tattered bricks or flagstones from mortared ones. Scrub away patio moss, pull out weeds from between bricks, and refill the space with sand to prevent future seeds from taking root.

These are not one-time fixes. Decks and patios require maintenance. Monitor them regularly for weeds and moss, and reseal decks occasionally.

ASK THE EXPERTS

I want to build a new deck. What sorts of restrictions can I expect?

Local code can dictate everything from building materials to the setback from the property line. Make sure that your deck is about two inches below the level of your home, or you may find rainwater washing into your living room. Decks 30 inches or higher from the ground need a railing to prevent accidental falls.

What's the difference between a sand and a mortar setting on a patio?

Sand settings are easier to install, so they're less expensive. Mortar settings, however, provide a firmer foundation that won't give way under heavy loads. They also don't allow weeds to grow between the bricks or stone.

How much time and money should I estimate for a deck or patio?

You can add a deck or patio with the help of family and friends in a weekend. Materials for a deck cost about $6 to $8 per square foot and for a patio under $3 per square foot. The cost of labor, of course, is another story entirely.

safety-smart grilling

Nothing says "home" like your first barbecue on the deck or patio of your new house. As fun as it is, grilling also requires some important safety precautions:

Site it right   When setting up your grill, place it on level ground in a well-ventilated area away from anything that could catch fire from floating sparks—including trees and shrubs.

Make sure your grill is scraped clean before you start   Brush or spray the grid with vegetable oil before lighting the grill.

Always lift the lid of a gas grill before lighting it   Leaving the lid down can result in a gas buildup and, yes, an explosion.

Never leave your grill unattended   It can become very hot, making the grill zone off-limits to children and pets.

Get a fire extinguisher and a spray bottle   Make sure you have a fire extinguisher handy—and that you know how to use it. Failing that, have a box of salt on hand to extinguish grease fires. A spritz of water from a spray bottle can help control flare-ups.

Use lighter fluid properly   If you use lighter fluid with a charcoal grill, make sure to store it far from the fire and away from young children and pets. Also, never squirt lighter fluid onto lit coals—the flame can travel up the stream to your hand.

Turn off a gas grill twice   Make sure you shut off a gas grill at the burner as well as at the tank.

Dress smart   Make sure your hair and clothing are grill-safe. Wear grill gloves, tie back long hair, and don't wear loose clothing that could brush up against the firebox. Sandals and open-toe shoes put you at risk for burned toes from dripping grease or falling embers.

THE WORKHORSES OF MOST BACKYARD BARBECUES

Charcoal Grills

The most common charcoal grill is the bowl-shaped **kettle-style grill.** The glowing coals rest on the bottom grate of the firebox, or "kettle," and a **grill grid** (also called a cooking grid) above the fire holds the food. Many grillers wouldn't dream of using anything but a charcoal grill, touting its advantages over the gas grill: Charcoal burns hotter, it gives food more of a "grilled" taste, and it's easy to add wood chunks or herbs to impart a smokier flavor. These grills cost from about $30 for a small portable to $450 for a large model with a rolling cart.

Gas Grills

Convenience is the name of the game with gas grills, because all you have to do is turn a knob to control the intensity of the flame. A quality gas grill, unlike a charcoal grill, will maintain a consistent temperature for hours. Gas grills are also cleaner to use: Most come with a catch pan built in under the firebox to gather grease. Propane is the fuel used with most gas grills. The propane cylinder will have to be replaced periodically.

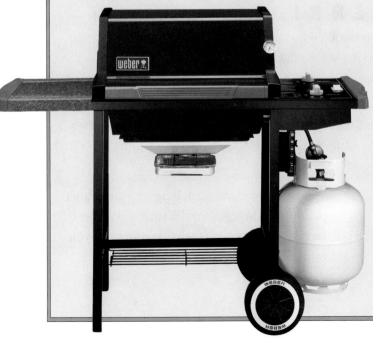

fences and walls

Make it sturdy— and legal

Good fences make good neighbors, or so the poem goes. Now that you are a homeowner, you just may learn the hard way what the poet was trying to say. Bad fences—those that are dilapidated or simply in the wrong place—can really annoy your neighbors. That's why you should inspect fences on your property carefully and make any necessary repairs soon after you move in. Signs that your fence needs repair include a sagging section of chain link or a wooden slat that's askew. Severe problems, such

as a rotted fence post, might require professional help. (If you need to find a contractor, see page 124.) The same goes for **retaining walls.** These are masonry or wooden walls that hold back dirt on sloping ground. A tilting retaining wall can spell trouble.

Don't plan on handling such projects over a weekend. Fences and walls require planning. The placement of a new wall or fence is usually pretty obvious. Walls even out sloping terrain, and fences define a border— whether they're at the edge of your property or around a play area within.

It's a good idea to tell your neighbors about any future changes that will abut their property line. They will appreciate the consideration and may ease approval through local zoning boards, if a zoning variance is required.

ASK THE EXPERTS

Will local regulations affect what I can do with my fence?

Probably. Some can prevent you from installing a fence or limit its height. They can also dictate your choice of building materials, such as pickets or chain link. Some regions even mandate how much passersby can see through your fences. Others prevent you from building a wall with railroad ties. The regulations go on and on, so verify restrictions in your area with the building inspector before you start. Also, the custom in most places is to position the more attractive side of your fence toward your neighbors.

Are there any alternatives to fences?

Fences aren't the only means of defining the edge of your property. Hedges do it equally well and also provide an ever-changing view. Although they may not require paint, hedges do require their own maintenance. Left unkempt by a previous owner, hedges can grow weedy in a few years. Planting a new hedge? Buy shrubs that will not grow too large, and don't plant them so close to the property line that they encroach on your neighbor's lot. It will take several years for your hedge to grow in. The results, however, will be delightful.

pools

In the swim

So you bought a home with a pool. Your inspection report should have noted whether your pool was in compliance with local ordinances. One of the most common regulations deals with the height of fences surrounding your pool (to prevent pets and unsupervised children from falling or jumping in). You must fix any fence problems noted by the inspector immediately.

Maintaining your pool is like taking out the trash: It's a regular task. Although you'll still want to check it visually every day, automatic mechanical devices can now handle regular upkeep, such as skimming out fallen leaves and removing oil and dirt. Regular maintenance will take about three hours a week.

ASK THE EXPERTS

What if I want to add a new pool?

Adding a pool to your yard costs money. The National Spa & Pool Institute estimates that aboveground pools cost $1,500 to $5,000—and that doesn't include the accessories that you'll require or want, such as a pool cover and fence. A basic in-ground pool, 15 feet by 30 feet, will cost between $16,000 and $20,000, plus the cost of accessories. Keep in mind that a pool can actually limit the attractiveness of your home to only those who will want to use it and who are willing to continue maintaining it. From a financial standpoint, you may barely recoup the money you invest. Where you live will drive this decision. A recent *Boston Globe* article noted that more New Englanders removed pools in a year than installed them.

Cleaning the pool

- Clean the tiles and walls (use a soft brush and pool-tile cleaner for tiles; follow manufacturers' suggestions for walls, which may be cement, vinyl, or fiberglass).

- Vacuum the pool at least once a week.

- Test the water regularly for chemical balance, especially if the water turns cloudy.

- Use a handheld leaf skimmer.

FIRST PERSON DISASTER STORY

MAINTENANCE BELLY FLOP

The pool was the last thing I thought about when I had to leave town to help my sister and her family in a crisis. Before I left, I placed the dogs with a sitter and asked my neighbor to water the garden. The pool? I just forgot about it. When I returned two weeks later, my pool had become a science experiment. Algae skimmed the surface. I quickly called a pool maintenance company to come out. They cleaned out the leaves and algae and loaded it up with noxious chemcals. The smell was overwhelming, but a week later I was finally able to use my pool again. Next time I go traveling, I've got a new item on my checklist: Hire a pool maintenance company.

—Bob L., New Smyrna Beach, Florida

kids outdoors

Be careful, so they can be carefree

If your property already has a fenced-in yard, young children will be well protected. Still, you should inspect your new property for hazards. A few improvements will make your kids' newfound paradise complete.

Designate spaces for romping that are in view of a frequently used room in your house, such as the kitchen. Did a swing set or jungle gym come with the house? Inspect them carefully before lettting the kids play on them. Loose parts might need new bolts. A new coat of paint can refresh rusted metal. Build or buy benches that can double as toy storage boxes to hold bats and balls. Pick up some pint-sized patio furniture—including chairs and a kids' table.

What you add to your garden requires equal consideration. You don't want your children to prick their skin, so don't plant bushes with thorns, such as roses or holly trees. Remove (or hire someone to extract) any poison ivy, oak, or sumac. Children will make forts under there. You don't want them coming in contact with these plants and suffering the effects.

ASK THE EXPERTS

Do swing sets and jungle gyms require padding?

That depends on your situation. The synthetic pads cropping up at public playgrounds help protect children from bruises and skinned knees. They also protect local governments from lawsuits. Grass in your backyard prevents scrapes (physical, not legal) as long as it's thick enough and you've cleared all rocks, protruding metal, and glass.

Aren't certain plants dangerous for kids to eat?

Absolutely, and for adults, too. That's why you need to make a thorough inspection of your yard when you buy a house. One option is to remove potential hazards before your child ingests them. Even if you do, make sure you teach your kids not to eat any growing plants and herbs.

What should I plant for my kids?

Let them choose plants, but guide them to those that excite their senses. Perhaps they'll choose one plant because it has a pretty flower or a soft and woolly touch, such as lamb's ears. Fragrant herbs such as rosemary and basil also go over well. A butterfly bush will attract butterflies and provide fun visual stimulation. These plants will also help your children look forward to your garden growing.

Should I forgo a sandbox if there are cats in the neighborhood?

You can keep the kitties at bay with a sandbox lid. Just make sure to close it tightly after your children finish playing. If you build your own box, you can convert it to a raised flowerbed once the kids outgrow making sand castles.

now what do I do?
Answers to common questions

Who can help me create a landscape plan?

A landscape architect can provide an overall plan for your future garden—even if you take years to implement it. Each architect has a style, so make sure you visit some previous clients to view finished designs before settling on an architect. If you're short on cash, call several larger nurseries in your area and ask them to send a representative out to give you a free estimate. Granted, they will probably recommend plants that they sell or have in large quantities in their inventory, but these plants will surely thrive since you share the same regional zone.

Can I plan a garden with my computer?

Yes. There are plenty of programs available, including SierraHome's Complete LandDesigner. It'll help you design the layout of your garden and even show you what it will look like five years from now when everything has grown in.

How much do trees and shrubs cost?

It depends on how old they are. You'll pay very little—frequently less than $20—for a tree or shrub that is only a foot or so tall. A mature 15-foot-tall flowering pear tree, however, might set you back several hundred dollars. Your budget will dictate whether to buy something that fits in immediately or takes longer to reach maturity. Good nurseries offer a one-year guarantee on their plants and trees.

How can I reduce my plant costs?

There are several options. You can plant more of your garden from seed, which requires advance planning. Order your seeds in midwinter, and start them in containers in February or March, before moving them outdoors after the final frost. Cost-conscious gardeners can also **propagate**—or clone—new plants from the stems of their existing ones. Just follow the directions found in most gardening books. For ready-to-plant flora, check out the spring sales of local gardening clubs. The selections are usually created from seed or propagation by local gardeners who know what works in your region, and they usually sell plants for significantly less than a nursery.

How can I keep my driveways and sidewalks from looking bad?

Maintain them. Asphalt, the blacktop used in many driveways, and concrete tend to crack with age. You can reseal asphalt and patch concrete but the results will be spotty. It's better to remove worn driveways and walks and then add new ones. It will cost more, but they will last for years and look great.

NOW WHERE DO I GO?!

CONTACTS

United States National Arboretum
Gardening site
**www.usna.usda.gov/Gardens/
gardeningr.html**

Department of Agriculture's Hardiness
Zone maps
www.usna.usda.gov/hardzone

List of cooperative extensions
for all 50 states
**landscaping.about.com/cs/
coopextension**

GardenWeb
(connection to various gardening online
discussion groups)
www.gardenweb.com

Better Homes and Gardens
(online version of the magazine)
www.bhg.com

The GardenHelper
(information for gardeners by gardeners)
www.thegardenhelper.com

BOOKS

National Audubon Society Field Guides
(Individual guides for various parts of the
country)
Alfred A. Knopf

The Outdoor Living Room
By Martha Baker

Deck and Patio Planner
John Riha

Home Maintenance for Dummies
By James Carey and James Morris

**Gardening 101: Learn How to Plan,
Plant, and Maintain a Garden**
By Martha Stewart, from The Best of
Martha Stewart Living

**The Four-Season Landscape: Easy-Care
Plants and Plans for Year-Round Color**
By Susan A. Roth

Decorating

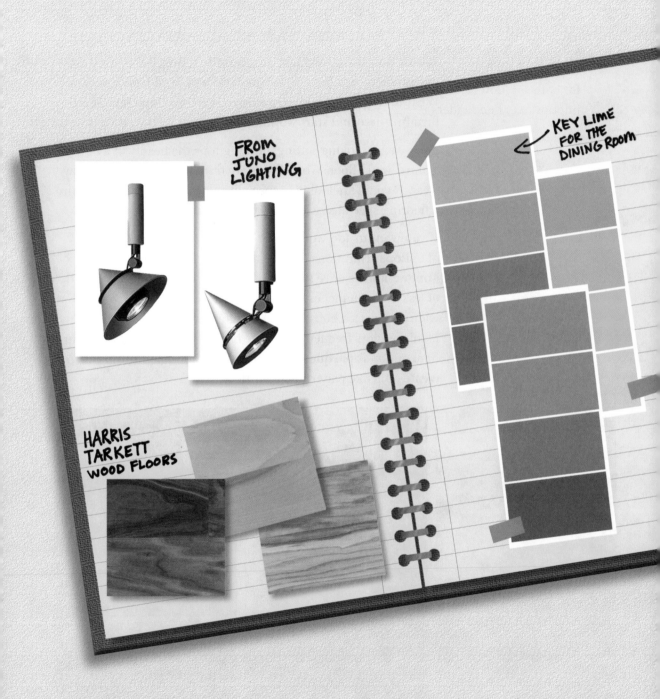

wood floors

On solid ground

Great, you've moved in, or are about to move. But there is only one problem: the floors. They're wood and need lots of work. What to do? If you can, keep those rooms with problem floors furniture-free and start working on them.

For a warm-looking setting, nothing tops the beauty of a newly stained wood floor. Wood floors are durable, but they still show wear. If yours are looking especially worn or scratched, then hire a flooring specialist who will sand and stain the floors.

If you want to add wood floors to your home, you've got plenty of options. Traditional wood flooring comes in three forms. **Tongue-and-groove strips** are the most common, with a width of less than 3¹/₄ inches. **Wide-plank flooring** is 4 or more inches wide and gives a house an old-fashioned feel. (In fact, wide-plank vendors frequently salvage boards from old houses.) Your final option is **parquet,** which uses wood of different shapes to create a tilelike pattern on your floor.

ASK THE EXPERTS

What's the difference between softwood and hardwood?

Floors are either made of **softwood** (generally pine or other conifers) or **hardwood** (such as oak, walnut, and maple). As their names imply, hardwoods are firmer than softwoods, and they tend to resist dents more readily than low-grade pines. A professional can sand, restain, and seal hardwood floors with polyurethane or varnish so they'll retain their good looks for years to come. Some softwoods, such as firs, refinish nicely, with beautiful variations in their grain. Others, however, may not be worth the expense of restaining. Instead, you might want to consider painting the floors and using a stencil to add decorative touches.

How can I tell if wood floors lie underneath wall-to-wall carpeting?

Do a little sleuthing. Are there wood floors in other parts of the house? If so, you're likely to find them under the carpeting. Pull up the wall-to-wall carpeting in an out-of-the-way corner. Find plywood? Keep digging. Cut a small corner of the plywood and pull it up as well. Plywood is sometimes placed over wood floors to give carpeting a more even surface.

Can I refinish floors myself?

Yes, but it's hard work. Rental centers can provide the sander you'll need. Home improvement stores and lumberyards carry the stains and sealant. Read up on refinishing techniques before diving into your project, however, or you'll end up with a sloppy finish.

carpeting and rugs

Stylish, quiet, and warm

Not every home has hardwood floors, and even fewer have beautiful ones. That's why there is carpeting. Carpeting can reduce echoes, help keep heating costs down, and also mask a world of troubles in your floors.

How you use floor coverings depends on your decorating style. Wall-to-wall carpeting tends to hide dirt better than area rugs. Wall-to-wall can also soften falls by children or an elderly parent. Area rugs come in more patterns and can be used like a piece of art when decorating a room.

Regardless of which carpet you choose, follow certain selection criteria. The Carpet and Rug Institute's performance rating system grades carpets from 1 (least resistant to wear) to 5 (most resistant). Select heavy-duty carpeting in heavy-traffic areas such as the family room, stairs, and children's rooms.

Save the more plush-pile carpet for the rooms that get less use, like the living and dining rooms and the master bedroom.

Choose your carpet: A. loop pile; B. cut pile; or C. cut and loop pile. You can also select area rugs, as shown in D.

164

ASK THE EXPERTS

What is pile?

Pile is the fabric face of the carpet (in other words, the side that sticks up into the room). There are three primary choices. In **loop pile,** the yarn loops back into the carpet's backing. In **cut pile,** these loops are sliced off. A third type, **cut and loop pile** provides a little of each. Your choice matters for aesthetic and practical reasons. Cut piles are softer, but loops tend to hide footprints better. Loops also catch animal claws, so they'll damage readily if your pet scratches.

What is padding?

Padding lies under your carpet and cushions your feet as you walk across a room. It also reduces wear and tear on your carpet—so buying a poorly constructed, inexpensive pad can end up costing you more. If you're installing new carpeting, always make sure you install a new pad at the same time. A plush pad that feels like you're walking on a soft lawn is best in lightly traveled bedrooms. Thinner pads work best in hallways. Depending on your carpet's pile, however, your pad should be no thicker than $3/8$ to $7/16$ of an inch. No matter what you decide, invest in good quality padding.

FIRST PERSON DISASTER STORY

PAD THE BILL

Everyone warned me about the temptation to save money on carpet by skimping on carpet padding. But did I listen? Absolutely not. I chose a lower-grade padding so I could get a higher quality carpet for our den. As soon as the installers were done, I knew that I'd made a mistake. Walking into the den felt about as comfortable as walking on marble. Worse, now I know that a bad pad can decrease the life of your carpet by half. My partner and I will fix this goof by replacing this carpet sooner than we planned—and by learning from the experience.

—Marian A., Minneapolis, Minnesota

paint

Your family coat

You've finally started to feel at home in your new house. Now it's time to make some improvements that add your style. Take a look around. Are there any rooms that could use either a fresh coat of paint in the same color or a whole new color treatment? You decide. Get those paint swatches and start imagining a room makeover. When you've settled on two or three colors you think might work, buy a quart of each and paint a 4-inch-square patch of each on the wall. Let it dry and then look at the patches at different times of the day. Do you still like the color at dusk? How about in the evening? In the morning? Paint looks different in different light, so try a bit out and see how it looks throughout the day and night.

The basic rules for painting both the inside and outside of your home are the same: You want to start high and work your way down. This ensures that paint doesn't drip on your completed sections. For a room, that means the ceiling first, followed by any **crown molding** (decorative trim between the ceiling and the walls), walls, doors, and door and window frames, and finally baseboards.

If you're interested in moving beyond a roller and paintbrush, you might try **sponging,** which uses an irregularly textured sponge for a decorative finish; **stamping,** which uses a rubber stamp, or **stenciling,** which is useful for borders. Painting the outside of your house is a larger undertaking (see "Exterior Improvements" on page 128).

ASK THE EXPERTS

What type of paint do I need?

Choose your paint based on a room's use. There are four major types of paint: gloss, semigloss, satin, and flat. **Gloss** paint is shiny and easiest to clean. It works well on trim where fingers can leave smudges. **Semigloss** still has enough sheen to make it readily washable, so you'll find it on the walls of kitchens and bathrooms. **Satin** and **flat** paint have progressively less gloss. They're more difficult to clean but can be perfect for the walls of your living or dining room.

Should I use oil or latex paint?

At one time, oil-based paint was considered to be better for exteriors and trim, but no more. Chemists have improved the ability of latex paints to work well in all environments. Oil smells worse, yellows with age, and is more difficult to clean. It also requires paint thinner to clean, whereas latex washes off with water. Choose latex whenever possible.

How much paint do I need?

That depends on the paint. A gallon of good paint can cover up to 400 square feet. Not-so-good paint covers significantly less—enough to eliminate the cost advantage. Calculate how much paint you'll need by multiplying the height of each wall by its length. Add the walls and ceiling for a total. Take these numbers to a paint store and read the labels to see how much coverage to expect. You'll probably need two coats.

What tools do I need to paint?

Brushes and rollers, for starters. But read their labels carefully to make sure you choose those that fit your project. Brushes help with trim and a house's exterior. Rollers work best on ceilings and interior walls, but a roller that applies paint evenly on drywall won't do the same for stucco.

Smart paint

Grime happens. Whether from fingerprints or mildew, your paint will accumulate a series of insults. So make the inevitable cleanup easier by selecting the correct paint in advance. For bathrooms, get mildew-resistant paint. Kitchens, bathrooms, and entrance doors will wipe cleaner with a gloss or semigloss paint.

wallpaper

Covering the walls

If you thought choosing a paint color was stressful, wait until you go looking for new wallpaper! The good news is that while wallpaper may cost more initially than paint, it lasts much longer. Wallpaper also hides stubborn cracks in old plaster, although you should still repair the wall surface before installing the paper.

The first rule about **wallpaper** or wallcovering (as it is sometimes called) is to match the room to the paper. You can choose vinyl, paper, foil, silk, and even wood chips. A bathroom's covering needs to be washed frequently, so silk won't do well there. Save it for a dining room, where it will look lovely, and use vinyl for the bathroom and kitchen.

When choosing your **pattern,** keep some basic principles in mind. Small patterns or broad stripes work best in rooms where you'll be hanging prints or photos. Broad stripes and bold patterns also help scale a huge room down to size, but they'll make a small room feel too claustrophobic.

Finally, check carefully that the rolls match. Wallpaper is printed in batches, and one might be slightly different from the next. The last thing you want is a room with two-tone wallpaper that you intended to be a perfect match.

There are scores of online sources for wallpaper, including **www.wallpetals.com.** Home Depot and Sherwin Williams also carry multiple options for all price ranges.

ASK THE EXPERTS

How much wallpaper will I need?

Wallpaper is usually sold in double rolls that cover a total of 56 feet. That's enough to cover a 7-foot section of a wall with 8-foot ceilings—if you make no errors. Measure the walls you want to cover. Buy at least one roll more than you'll need to allow for mistakes and for working around window frames and angles.

What if I don't think I can handle the wallpapering myself?

Wallpaper looks so easy to put up and yet goes wrong so frequently. Patience and a careful eye will ensure that your papered room looks great. If that doesn't comfort you, hire a professional. As with all services, you should get at least three price quotes.

What is peelable wallpaper?

Whether you're preparing to put up new paper or merely exposing your walls for paint, stripping any existing wallpaper is a crucial first step to the walls you desire. If your house has strippable or peelable wallpaper, you're in luck. Simply pull the sheets off the walls with both hands. Peelable paper leaves a thin paper backing on the wall that you can remove with soap and hot water.

What if my wallpaper isn't peelable?

Score the paper using a wallpaper removal tool called a "paper tiger," which pokes small holes in the paper. Next, spray an ammonia-based solution, such as Windex, on the paper and let it sit for 15 minutes. Start at a corner and it should peel off. If not, use a standard putty knife to help it come off. Alternatively, you can rent a **wallpaper steamer.** It applies the same principal, but with less fuss. This mini-humidifier applies moisture directly to the wall—loosening the paper so you can remove it with ease.

Panic Attack

Is it just me or does everyone feel like screaming after one hour looking at wallpaper samples? I have never felt so overwhelmed in my life. So many choices, so many varieties. White paint is starting to look good again. One possibility: I can bring in an interior designer on a limited basis. Or I can ask a creative friend whose style I like.

tiling

A mosaic of decorating options

Tiles are simultaneously functional and elegant. Best of all, they make a room easier to clean—which is why you find them in bathrooms, kitchens, and entry halls. You can combine tiles in geometric shapes or place individual tiles in a design to add color. Tiles are also versatile: You can put them on your floors, walls, or countertops.

Tiles come in three main varieties. **Field tiles** (A) are the principal tiles used in a setting; they can be square or hexagonal. **Trim tiles** (B) provide accents—whether they're 1-inch-wide tiles that border square field tiles or small squares that fit between hexagonal ones. **Bullnose tiles** (C) are rounded for edges or can provide a smooth transition from tile to bare wall (D).

As you select tiles, keep in mind that floor tiles are sturdier than wall tiles. (You can use an attractive floor tile on a wall.) A wall tile, however, won't stand up to foot traffic. For both types of tile, **grout,** a thin type of mortar, fills in the crevices between tiles. Applying a sealer to the tiles and grout helps make the floor, wall, or countertop easier to clean. Grout can also be an important design element. Grout comes in many different colors, including various shades of white, beige, gray, and even black. Your grout complements your tile choice, or it can even make a design statement all its own. For instance, using black grout with plain white tiles creates a dramatic look.

ASK THE EXPERTS

How can I clean the tiles in our new house?

You can clean the tiles themselves with soap, water, and elbow grease. The grout between tiles is usually what causes tiles to look cruddy. Regrouting the tiles will freshen up the room in no time. Get a grout remover (a simple can opener will do) to pick out dirty grout down to a level sufficient for new grout to fill, about one-eighth to one-quarter inch. Make sure to regrout the entire floor or bathtub, because your new grout will probably differ in color from the existing one.

Can I install tiles?

Yes. Wall and counter tiles are the easiest to install yourself. It's important to keep in mind, however, that the difficulty of the task depends on the design and workspace. However, laying a tile floor, especially in a bathroom, can be difficult, because of cutting odd angles around fixtures. Here it's best to hire a professional.

What is an underlayment?

Floor tiles rest on top of two layers (three if you include the subfloor). An **underlayment,** generally a cement backer board, creates a rigid backing that sits on top of the more flexible wood subfloor. By removing the bounce of a wood floor, you're eliminating the chance your tile floor will crack. Adhesive (either **mastic** or **thinset mortar**) lies on top of the underlayment and holds your tiles in place. Since you don't walk on them, wall or countertop tiles stick directly to the surface with mastic (no backer board or thinset is necessary).

I hate the color of my tile's grout. What can I do?

You can remove the grout and start with a new color. Or, if the grout is in good condition, paint over the old grout with a grout colorant. There are a variety of colors to choose from.

lighting

Brightening your days

Few things are as important or as frequently overlooked in home decorating as lighting. A poorly lit room obscures all your decorating handiwork, makes working at a desk more tiresome, and can negatively affect your mood.

First, take an inventory of what you've already got. Look at the fixtures (ceiling lights and sconces) that came with your house as well as the lamps that you brought. Judge your lights on how well they light a room, not just on whether the fixtures themselves look attractive.

Different rooms require different amounts of light. Kitchens and other work areas need to be bright. A living room can be dimmer. **Ambient,** or indirect, light is softer than direct light. Ambient light is reflected off walls or ceilings, or from a **sconce** (a wall-mounted lamp) casting its light on the wall. By contrast, **accent** or **task** lighting is light that illuminates directly: A swing-arm lamp can light your reading material while you sit on a sofa, and track lighting can make it easier to see the lemons you are cutting.

ASK THE EXPERTS

Won't using a lot of lights run up my electric bill?

Yes. Fortunately, manufacturers now produce energy-saving fluorescent replacement bulbs for incandescent lights. These consume significantly less energy while keeping your home well lit. Some have filters to give the appearance of a soft-white incandescent bulb.

Isn't fluorescent light ugly?

Incandescent bulbs—the traditional light source in American homes—cast a warm yellow glow in a room. **Halogen** bulbs give a whiter light that is closer to natural sunlight. **Fluorescent** bulbs have a lingering reputation for a nasty bluish light, but modern fluorescents come closer to matching incandescent bulbs, with filters giving off some of the same soft glow. These subtle differences change the way colors look in a room. That makes it essential to look at fabric and paint samples under the same light source you'll use at home. If you've already decorated your interior, try different light sources to see which works best with your colors.

What should I do if a room is both a workspace and a more casual gathering spot?

Help your lights do double duty by installing a dimmer switch. Just keep in mind that a dimmer works only with incandescent and halogen bulbs. Fluorescent bulbs have two settings: on and off.

Should I consider candles in my lighting scheme?

Absolutely—and natural-oil lamps, too. Candle sconces and hurricane lamps help give a home an old-time feel. These work best in your dining room or other spaces where subdued light helps create a romantic atmosphere. However, if you use candles, also use caution, especially if children or pets are in your home. Never leave lit candles unattended.

Keep it light

Use light in your room designs. When you buy your house, you'll have two immediate sources of lighting: the sun and mounted fixtures. Think about how the room looks at different times of the day—and particularly at night.

Rooms with couches need direct light for reading. You can add lamps on side tables, set out floor lamps, or mount new swinging lamps from the walls. Televisions and computer monitors, however, frequently reflect direct light, which can cause eyestrain. For these settings, try indirect, or ambient, light. You can get this effect by bouncing light off a wall or ceiling with sconces, spotlights, or floor lamps. They can help lighten up a room without causing glare.

furniture

The finishing touch

This will inevitably happen, so don't panic. You've moved in and you've started to put your furniture in the right rooms—and suddenly it's not quite right anymore. And then it hits you: You've just spent all this money on the house, only to realize that your old furniture won't work in it. What to do?

Before buying more furniture, define your needs. Start with the basics (sleeping and eating). For instance, you already have a bed, but may lack side tables or lamps for bedtime reading. You may have a couch, but no armchairs. Create a list of what you need. Rate the importance of each piece to prioritize your shopping and help you manage your budget.

Measure your house and create a floor plan using 8$\frac{1}{2}$-by-11-inch graph paper (where each square on the graph equals 1 foot). Make scale templates of your existing furniture to create a layout and start figuring out the best place to put individual pieces. This can help you determine what size furniture will fit in your new home.

Of course, buying furniture is expensive. Create an overall idea of what you want a room to look like and buy quality pieces to fit the holes in your plan. Let it evolve over time—for instance, you can add an antique to contrast with an otherwise modern design.

Making old furniture new again

Buying a house has a way of making old furniture come out of the woodwork. Relatives suddenly realize that the chair sitting in their garage or their old couch is just the thing you need. (Never mind the bright orange fabric that relegated it to storage in the first place.)

Some pieces are just not worth the expense of changing the fabric. A good quality sofa, however, can set you back as much as $5,000. Inherit one with a solid frame and you can reupholster it for a fraction of that cost. Family heirlooms are generally worth the expense just for the sentimental value. Plus, older furniture often contains carved wood or other details you won't find in pieces made today.

Take a good look at the fabric. If it's not too worn and you enjoy the color and design, consider having it cleaned. If the springs and padding are fine, a slipcover can spruce up a chair or couch without the extra cost of having it reupholstered.

Of course, sometimes reupholstering is the only option. You need to decide whether you'll hire a pro (and whether to work with an interior designer) or brave the risks of botching the job and do it yourself. Regardless, fabric shops such as Calico Corners can help you find material at a discount that will help trim your costs.

now what do I do?
Answers to common questions

Can I plan my decorating on my computer?

Yes. Among other programs, FloorPlan 3D Design Suite 4.0 is available for both Windows and Macintosh operating systems. It lets you design your interior and then renders it in 3-D graphics.

How can I decide on the colors for a room?

Stores from Wal-Mart to Home Depot provide color-matching services. They can custom-mix paint that will match your existing color scheme. Books such as *The Decoration of Houses* by Alexandra Stoddard recommend classic color schemes that will meet the approval of the fiercest color snobs. You can also hire an interior decorator to help you decide.

When should I choose a decorator?

As soon as you find it difficult to make any decisions, hiring a decorator is a wise move. Look for local decorators at the American Society of Interior Designers' Web site at **www.interiors.org.** Interview several designers, making sure you look over examples of their past work. Ask for references from recent clients and call them to see how the decorator fared. Also, be sure to be as specific as you can about your needs. For example, you can hire a decorator to help you only with your color scheme while making your own decisions about furniture (other than fabrics).

If we're refinishing floors, how quickly can we move in?

Refinished wood floors require an absolute minimum of 48 hours—and you'll still smell the vapors. Better to budget three days for the floors to dry before you move in. If you're refinishing them after you move in, you'll have to get out of the house for the same amount of time (it's a great time for a vacation). You can walk on a painted or tiled floor 24 hours after it's done. Wait at least 72 hours before placing furniture on the floor.

I love the look of hardwood floors. But they require such care. Is there an easier way?

Try installing laminates—flooring strips made of wood-based products. Laminates are prefinished, so installation is your main concern. They're also thinner than traditional wood floors (seven-eighths of an inch), making them ideal for covering older flooring without having to raise the floor.

What is feng shui?

It is the ancient Chinese tradition of ordering a room for harmony. It translates as "wind, water." Feng shui principles suggest that good design allows energy to flow like the wind. If energy is blocked by poorly placed walls or furniture, it stagnates, like standing water. You can find out more about feng shui in books or do research online. You can also hire a feng shui consultant to review your home.

Should I buy new carpeting or clean the old?

If you like the carpeting, try cleaning it first. It's a lot less expensive than putting down new carpeting. You can hire a carpet cleaning service. Or you can do it yourself, rent a carpet cleaner, and follow the rental company's advice.

NOW WHERE DO I GO?!

CONTACTS

National Wood Flooring Association
(Search engine of members directs you to sources for installation and refinishing)
www.woodfloors.org

The Carpet and Rug Institute
(Database of CRI-qualified installers)
www.carpet-rug.com

PaintInfo.org
(Consumer information from the National Paint & Coatings Association)
www.paintinfo.org

International Association of Lighting Designers
(Searchable database of professionals)
www.iald.org

BOOKS

The Decoration of Houses
By Alexandra Stoddard

Use What You Have Decorating
By Lauri Ward

The Perfect Palette: Fifty Inspired Color Plans for Painting Every Room in Your Home
By Bonnie Rosser Krims

Selling your house

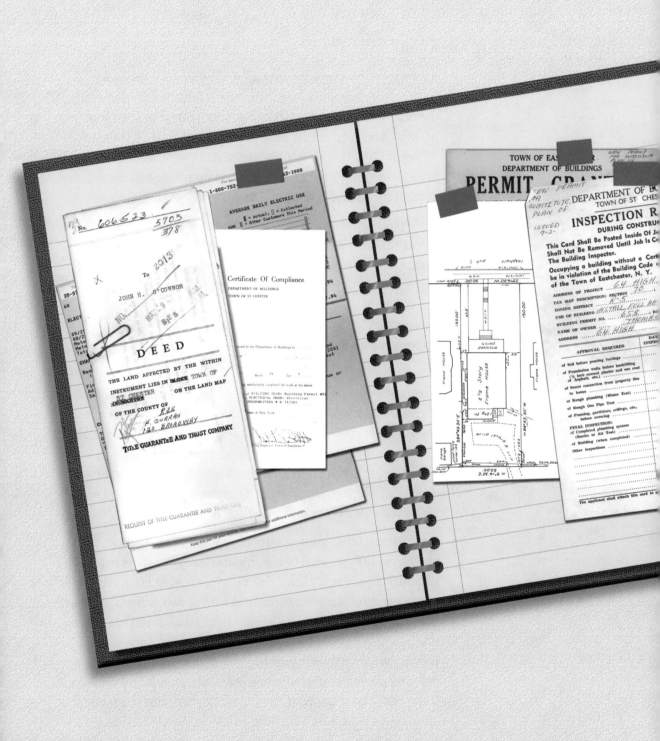

on the market

How a house gets sold

So you've decided to put your home on the market. For some, it's a simple business transaction. For others, it's the most wrenching, emotional experience of their lives. In either case, the easiest way to do it is to hire a licensed real estate agent or broker. (See page 182 for questions to ask an agent.) What does an agent do? First, she will help you determine the right selling price based on recent sales of local **comparable homes** (homes of similar size and construction in your neighborhood).

Once your house has been priced, the agent will write up a sales report on the house that is then available to other agents. Most agents also will host an **open house,** where other agents can come and see the house first before it officially goes on the market. After the open house, the agency will likely place ads in newspapers (at its expense) about your house. The agent will be responsible for showing your house to prospective customers.

How do you find an agent? Nearly all real estate agents work for a real estate agency. If you don't know an agent, ask family, friends, and coworkers for referrals, or simply walk into a local real estate agency and ask to speak with a broker. While you're there, take a look at their **listings** (a list of homes for sale, noting prices, special features, and addresses). You can either choose an agent yourself or the agency will assign one to work with you. This person will be called the **listing agent.**

Keep in mind that selling your house usually takes longer than buying one. If you need to move, start the sale process before you go hunting for a new home. Selling while buying is complicated, not to mention stressful. It requires timing two difficult transactions to happen at pretty much the same time. If you're worried that you won't have enough time to find a house once you sell yours, you can include a **contingency clause** in the sale contract delaying closing until you have a contract to buy a house. Don't insist on it—you may be better off renting a place for a few months after you've sold than to risk losing a sale. Likewise, attorneys for buyers in some regions will not accept such a clause.

ASK THE EXPERTS

Is it ever better to rent out your house, rather than sell it?

In a very poor housing market, it just doesn't make sense to sell. Your house is probably your single biggest investment. Rather than see that investment shrink by cashing out, think about renting it out while you wait for the housing market in your area to improve. Renting has its drawbacks, though. For one, your money remains locked up in the house—which might prevent you from buying another home. Also, renters generally don't have an incentive to maintain a house, which can cause it to look run-down. Ideally, you want renters who'll like your house enough to want to buy it. Offer them a lease with an option to buy. That way they'll have a greater sense of ownership—even before buying—and they'll keep your investment in better shape.

FIRST PERSON DISASTER STORY

NO WONDER THEY CALL IT "OPEN HOUSE"

There's a reason why agents tell you not to be home when they show your house. But on this particular day I couldn't get away, and I happened to be upstairs when a steady stream of potential buyers arrived. Even though I couldn't wait to move, I was having a hard time letting go of the first home we ever bought—so many memories! I couldn't help but listen, waiting to hear comments about the charm of the entry and the appeal of the rest of the house. Then came the shock. Instead of fawning, these strangers said things like, "They'll never get what they're asking." "Maybe wallpaper will help these rooms." "You could lose the garden to add a deck." All I could think was, "How could they?" Lesson learned: Leave. Get an ice-cream sundae, see a movie, buy things for the new house, visit friends or relatives. Be anywhere but your home during an open house, away from those strangers who will say the strangest, most untrue things about your perfect home.

—Anne V., Huntington, New York

hiring an agent

The right marketer can make a difference

To sell your house, a real estate agent needs plenty of marketing savvy. Agents sell your house for a percentage of the total sale price (see page 30). The bigger the sale price, the bigger the fee. This is a good thing, because they're motivated to get you top dollar. That's why you need to interview several potential agents to discuss selling (or listing) your house. Ask them how they plan on marketing your home. Will they have open houses? Will there be ads in the local newspaper? Do they think current market conditions make it a good time to sell? Ask if they are full- or part-time agents and for details on their sales production.

Once you choose a real estate agent, he will ask you to sign a **listing agreement.** This is a contract between you and the real estate agency. It states how long the agent will work for you (typically three to six months) and, more important, the terms and the commission the agent will receive. That commission is usually a percentage of the sale price and will likely be in the 4% to 6% range, payable upon closing. A broker may establish a commission rate for agents in its office, but it is illegal for companies to agree to charge a single rate.

There are three basic types of agreements. The first is called an **open listing;** here the seller agrees to pay the agent only if the agent finds a buyer. The second is an **exclusive listing,** meaning the agent is entitled to a commission even if you (or another agent) find the buyer for the house. Because the agent is assured some financial reward, he should list your house on various MLS databases (see page 32) available to any real estate agent to sell. With a multiple listing, if an agent from an unaffiliated real estate office finds a buyer for your home, that agent is due a portion (usually half) of your agent's commission. The last type is called an **office-exclusive listing**. This type of agreement allows only the broker or his office associates to sell your house; there is no MLS listing.

ASK THE EXPERTS

How long should I list my house with an agent?

Most agents will want six months' exclusivity; try to narrow that to 120 days or about four months. Why? It's a good idea to limit the contract to the shortest duration so you are not committed to staying with one broker for an unreasonable length of time.

What is a lockbox?

It's a little metal box with a combination lock that is locked to your doorknob. The lockbox holds the key to your front door. That way you only have to provide the listing agent with one key to your home. Your agent can give out the combination to other agents who are bringing prospective buyers to see your place, even if neither you nor your agent is available to show it.

My broker isn't doing a good job selling my home. Can I switch to a different agency or agent?

Once you list your property with a broker, you have to abide by your contract for its full term. For example, if you have a three-month listing agreement, you can't decide after a month to give the listing to another real estate agency—you have to wait until the listing expires. However, your contract is usually with the agency and not with a particular agent, so you can ask the manager of the real estate office to assign a new agent to your home sale.

I found a buyer myself while my house was on the market. Do I have to pay my broker anything?

You may still have to pay the broker a commission unless you and your broker already agreed in the listing agreement that the broker would accept a reduced commission if you found a buyer on your own.

negotiating a fee

The right price

Commission for an agent who sells your home ranges from about 4% to 6%. For a $146,000, median-priced house in America, sold by a broker that charges a 6% commission, that comes to $8,760. Yes, that's a nice chunk of change, but a good-sized portion of it will be shared with the agent's office to pay for overhead and expenses. Fortunately, you can negotiate the fee to some degree and save yourself cash that will help finance your next home.

Ask each agent that you interview what his fee is. Once you've narrowed the field of agents, go back to each. Ask if they'd be willing to take a smaller percentage. You're more likely to negotiate a lower fee in a hot real estate market with low inventory, when houses are flying off the table, and brokers don't have to work as hard to sell them. This happy state of affairs is called a seller's market. Often agents are more amenable to a lower fee if they know they can turn your house around quickly. The commission is negotiable until closing.

Bear in mind, however, that a listing agent typically splits the commission with another broker who brings in the purchaser. The agent often splits his fee with his agency, too. The listing agent also incurs costs on your behalf—such as advertising your house in the local paper's classified section, as well as printing costs for brochures, to say nothing of the gallons of gas spent driving prospective clients to see your house. This is not necessarily a lot of money, but it becomes especially significant in a slow market when ads have to run for weeks or months.

ASK THE EXPERTS

What can I do to negotiate a lower fee?

If you're hoping to save a little money, you might want to negotiate fewer services for a reduced commission. For example, you can pay for the classified ads and the flyers. In the end, however, keep in mind that reducing the commission can also reduce your agent's incentive to sell your house.

I've changed my mind and want to take my house off the market before the listing agreement expires. Can I do that?

Yes, but your real estate agency may expect reimbursement for advertising and other out-of-pocket costs. Also, if your broker has found a willing buyer at your price and you decide not to sell, you can be sued by the agent for damages, such as a lost commission or expenses incurred. You may be able to protect yourself if you insert a clause in the listing agreement that allows you to end the agreement if you change your mind about selling, or a clause that allows you to say no to any deal the broker presents to you for any reason. (However, many brokers won't agree to such conditions.)

What are "fee for service" or "à la carte" services?

To better fit the midrange of sellers' needs (and to give consumers the ability to lower their commission expenses by handling much of the sales process themselves), some brokers have unbundled their services and allow sellers to pick and choose the services they want.

selling it yourself

For sale by owner

If paying a broker thousands of dollars to sell your house gives you the willies, consider selling your house yourself. For sale by owner (also known as **FSBO**) is a common selling technique across the country. In fact, according to the National Association of Realtors, between 10% and 20% of all homes are sold by the owner. In 1999, the figure was 16%.

The major problem for most sellers is pricing their home correctly. You've got an emotional attachment that might blind you from seeing its flaws. You may also be so aggravated with your house's problems that you don't appreciate its advantages. Spend $200 and hire a professional house appraiser. Her report will give you a good idea of how much comparable homes are fetching nearby.

Once all the preliminaries are taken care of, it's time to market. Advertise your home through classified ads in the local paper, a "For Sale" sign out front, and word of mouth. Don't forget the power of e-mail: By listing the details and sending a note to your friends, they can forward it to their friends and the exposure grows exponentially. You can also post details of your home at several online sites for a monthly fee or pay a higher one-time fee to list your house until it sells. The informational Web site **www.audrie.com** lists the costs and options of several online FSBO advertising sites.

Welcome to *Audrie.com*

Prepare → Set Price → Close → Advertise → Show & Sell → Negotiate

audrie.com

Buying ? See:

Audrie's Advice for Buying a home

Calculate a mortgage payment

ASK THE EXPERTS

How can I ensure that a potential buyer is serious?

One way is to check if they have prequalified for a mortgage (see page 46).

When is the best time to sell my house?

In general, you'll get more buyers—and, hence, better prices—in spring and summer. People generally don't want to go out house hunting in nasty winter weather and during the holiday season. Parents are also loath to move during the school year, so they wait to make their move in the spring and summer. On the other hand, some buyers and sellers don't care what time of year it is. If you choose the less busy seasons of fall and winter, your home faces less competition from other properties.

Do I still need a lawyer if I sell the house myself?

Yes. In fact, before listing your house you need to consider any legal obstacles on your house that would foil a sale. These might be any tax or contractor liens that need to be paid, illegal additions that need local approval, ground contamination from a leaking oil tank that needs to be cleaned up, or asbestos that needs to be removed professionally. You're going to need a lawyer to review the **contract of sale** (the preliminary contract that both you and the buyer must sign). You will also need a lawyer to hold the buyer's deposit for you in escrow. And, of course, you will need a lawyer for the closing, so you might as well line one up at the beginning of the process to ensure good advice on any legal problems that you may incur during the sale.

getting to "Sold"

Preparing your house

You want to sell your home quickly so you can move into your new house, so think like a buyer. Address as many issues as possible before you put your house on the block.

Pull out the inspection report from when you bought the house. Check whether you've addressed any deficiencies listed then. Hire an engineer to give your home the once-over; he'll confirm or allay your suspicions, and probably nip some other problems in the bud. Plan to make improvements before showing the house. If you don't wish to correct any problems—for example, a broken washing machine—you can find out how much it would cost to fix it or buy a new one. You will then be prepared to deduct the correct amount from your asking price if a buyer insists on it.

The real problem in selling a house is the **asking price.** If you don't get any offers in the price range you want after the house has been on the market for 60 days you will need to lower your asking price. Another problem: ignoring low offers. Entertain all offers, and always counteroffer even if you receive a bid significantly under your asking price.

Panic Attack

Will they like the kitchen? I can't decide whether to put in a new dishwasher before I sell the house or not. I know—with new dishwasher racks, it won't look so old. New covers for the kitchen chairs will help too.

Organizing your house documents

To help speed the buying process, it's a good idea to put certain documents in order to show prospective buyers. Some documents will be needed before your agent will officially take on selling your house; others will be needed at the closing (see page 90).

- The **deed** to the house. This document proves that you were legally granted ownership of the house.

- The **title report** from your closing or, if you don't have that, the title insurance policy. This document shows that you're the legal owner of the house.

- A **survey** of the property—a map that shows your house and property.

- A **certificate of occupancy** and any other certificates documenting work you have had done on the house. If you did extensive renovations, this will show that the house has been inspected and is safe for occupancy.

- **Real estate tax bills** from the past two years.

- The most recent **mortgage statement**.

- The most recent **utilities statements**.

- If you're selling a condo, you'll need the condo declarations, bylaws, and the current rules and regulations. Also, get a **paid-up assessment letter** from the management company (or board treasurer) to show that your account is current.

smart selling tips

Give yourself every advantage

Now's the time to pull out every trick in the book to make your house look more inviting. Beautifully decorated, pristine houses are usually the first to sell. First, take care of the basics. Clean everything in your house: the floors, walls, doors, windows, and bathrooms. Make sure the towels in your bathroom are fresh and that they match. Don't leave pots and pans in your drain board. Put away the dishes in your dishwasher (potential owners will open it, so have it cleaned, too).

De-clutter as much as possible (put nonessentials in storage if necessary). And consider adding a fresh coat of paint if it's been a while since the last one.

Your house's exterior and yard need careful attention, too. Clean out the gutters so leaves are not poking over the top. Trim your hedges and edge your walks. Rake and mow the lawn. Even your garden needs to look nice. You should weed and mulch your flowerbeds. If your perennials are already done blooming for the year, add some annuals.

On the day of a viewing, give everything a final vacuuming and dusting. Clean the countertops of breadcrumbs. If you've got a cat, be sure to empty the litter box. For the crowning touches, put fresh-cut flowers in vases around your home and a potted plant outside the entrance to make a great first impression. Bake cookies or some bread to add pleasing aromas. If it's winter, light a fire in your fireplace to make it cozy.

Turn on lights around your house to give rooms instant appeal. You'll especially want to light up dark corners that make your rooms seem small. Finally, play jazz or classical music softly on your stereo. Just make sure it's a repeating CD or a looping tape so that it continues playing. This final aural intoxicant can help make your house seem like a home to prospective buyers.

ASK THE EXPERTS

Why do I need to make repairs that won't benefit me?

Buyers notice when you haven't taken care of basic maintenance on your house. Even little things like a screen window
that needs to be replaced can trigger questions about how well
you've handled the major maintenance. This fear has a cost—in
a lower price to cover anticipated repairs. Remove this fear and
you raise the asking price of your home. Plus, your home is competing with so many others—why risk making a bad impression
with something so easy to fix?

Can I let my house go between showings?

Don't count on it. Your agent may want to show the house on
a day's notice—or less. Keeping your house tidy and ready to be
seen on a few hours' notice means that you're accommodating
the customer. That's the key to selling anything—so plan on
keeping it up for a few weeks, even if you normally keep a more
casual home.

Can I have my dogs around during the showing?

You'll be better off boarding your dogs and cats with a neighbor or taking them with you when you vamoose during a showing. Your pet will put off people with allergies immediately.
Unfortunately, the backyard doesn't work as a substitute for
dogs either. Prospective buyers will want to inspect the yard, and
even the friendliest of dogs can scare off the canine-phobic.

How can I make sure that my house is looking its best?

After you've done everything you can imagine, have your
agent and a friend give it the once-over. They can act as substi-
tutes for potential buyers. Ask them to be brutal, and don't be
annoyed when they point out problems. They're doing you a
favor, not criticizing your homemaking capabilities.

the selling process

The timeline of a sale

The first house you buy is rarely the only home that you'll own. You may have settled for a home too small for your growing family, or gotten a new job that is too far from your current home. In any case, it's time to move on.

No doubt you remember many parts of the process from when you bought your last home, and you can learn from that experience. Remember what you looked for as a buyer, and keep in mind the little things you can do to make the transaction go smoothly.

Before you put your house on the market:

■ Research the current value of houses in your neighborhood. Check out the Web site **www.realtor.com** to get comparable values for similar homes in your area.

■ Review the original inspection report from when you purchased the house to confirm that you've addressed any deficiencies.

■ Fix any other problems and paint the interior to make the house look fresh.

■ Rent a room in a storage facility where you can put any extra furniture or boxes that clutter up your house.

■ Make photocopies of your utility bills from both the summer and winter to provide prospective buyers with a sense of how much your house costs to run.

■ Investigate whether you'd be willing to go without an agent and handle a For Sale By Owner.

■ Interview agents, get the numbers of their past clients, and call these references.

■ Negotiate the agent's fee.

■ Determine a price for listing the house, using either the broker's knowledge or your research of the market.

Once you've put your house on the market:

■ Clean the house inside and out, including vacuuming, mowing the lawn, and trimming the hedges.

■ On days the agent shows the house, take all your pots and pans out of the drain board, empty the dishwasher, take out the trash, and place fresh flowers around the house and a plant outside the entrance, perhaps on the top step.

■ Select a lawyer to handle your closing, negotiating a reduced fee if she'll also handle the purchase of your next home.

■ Begin your search for a new home.

Once you receive a bid:

■ Get as much information from the buyer as possible about their financial qualifications, whether they have a home to sell, and when they can close.

■ Negotiate the offer.

■ Tell your attorney to prepare a contract and to send it to the buyer's lawyer.

■ Have several copies of your property survey on hand to speed up the title insurance report on the buyer's end. Banks always require a copy of the survey, too.

■ Start looking for a new home, or determine where you'll rent after the closing.

■ Coordinate a closing date that is convenient for both parties and set your moving date accordingly.

now what do I do?

Answers to common questions

What should a broker's Web site contain?

There are certain basics that need to be included, such as the agent's phone number and e-mail address so prospects know how to reach her. But there are more subtle clues that can tell you whether the agent is serious about using the Internet. Make sure that the properties listed are up-to-date. Old properties indicate a site that's been neglected, which means your agent doesn't seriously think the Internet is a good place for prospects.

Can a purchaser take over my mortgage?

That depends on the terms of your mortgage. Check with your bank to see whether it is assumable. If so, the obligation to pay the mortgage can be handed over to the buyer. While it takes some time to get a bank's O.K., this is an appealing financial trick when your existing mortgage has a low interest rate and current rates are high. It can also save the buyer money on any mortgage tax, which you paid when you bought the house. Generally, the buyer pays you the difference between the purchase price and the mortgage in a combination of cash (the deposit) and a second mortgage.

What kinds of things can go wrong between the signing of the contract and the closing?

Unfortunately, many things can happen. On the closing day, it's customary to have an inspection of the house. This way if the buyer finds an unexpected problem, like a flooded basement, both parties will be faced with the decision as to whether they should cancel the deal (assuming the condition would create proper grounds for the buyer to back out of the contract) or renegotiate the terms of the deal in light of the new discovery. Problems with financing are also common. If the buyer's financing didn't come through or didn't come through in time, the parties will have to decide whether to cancel the purchase agreement or delay the closing.

I'm selling my house myself. What should I put on the "For Sale" sign?

It should include everything that an agent might provide. Instead of an agent's name, it should say "For Sale By Owner." List your phone number and note that your house will be shown by appointment only—unless you're planning on an open house. For a fee, you can post photos of your home at the Web site For Internet Sale By Owner (**www.fisbo.com**).

NOW WHERE DO I GO?!

CONTACTS

National Association of Realtors
www.Realtor.com

Audrie.com
(Advice on selling your home yourself)
www.audrie.com

For Internet Sale By Owner
www.fisbo.com

BOOKS

Seller Beware: Insider Secrets You Need to Know About Selling Your House—From Listing Through Closing the Deal
By Robert Irwin

How to Sell Your Home Fast, for the Highest Price, in Any Market
By Terry Eilers

100 Surefire Improvements to Sell Your House Faster
By R. Dodge Woodson

How to Sell Your Own Home: The Practical Homeowner's Guide to Selling by Owner
By William F. Supple

glossary

Acre
A measurement for property. One acre equals 43,560 square feet. The median lot size for the United States is one-third of an acre.

Adjustable rate mortgage (ARM)
A loan with an interest rate that varies over time. ARM rates are set for a period of one to seven years and then convert to the then-prevailing market rate. ARM's typically have lower rates than 30-year mortgages, so they help reduce cost when rates are high.

Agent
A house salesperson. Agents show you houses and earn a commission from the seller.

Annual percentage rate (APR)
A number that indicates the true total cost of a mortgage, including the interest rate, points, and any fees.

Asbestos
Once a common form of insulation for hot-water pipes. Frequently removed by specialists if frayed, but left in place if properly sealed.

Assessed value
The value that a county or state places on a house as the basis for determining property taxes. Generally, assessments run less than the actual cost of a house (see **Market value**).

Assessment
An extra common charge in a condo or co-op to pay for unanticipated expenses, such as storm damage.

Assets
How a banker measures the value of your possessions, such as money or cars, and commitments due to you, such as salary or alimony. Assets are offset by **liabilities** to determine your net worth.

Bid
The offer of how much you're willing to pay for a house.

Binder agreement
A less-than-stringent legal document used in some parts of the country to tie a buyer to a purchase. These documents frequently provide the seller with "wiggle room" to back out of the deal until the real contract is signed.

Building inspectors
Local officials who inspect changes to homes to ensure they conform to local building codes. The inspector has to sign off on any improvements before you can get a certificate of occupancy (see **Home inspector**).

Building permit
Approval from the building inspector to go ahead with improvements to your home. Whether you require one depends on the extent of the changes and on local laws.

Certificate of occupancy (CO's)
The local government's seal of approval that a house is fit for habitation. Only houses with up-to-date COs are legal residences—which your lawyer will verify as part of your purchase.

Closing
The meeting in which you sign the legal documents and pay the fees completing the purchase.

Closing costs
What a bank charges you to cover its costs in providing a mortgage, including everything from the bank attorney's fee to copying costs for the required paperwork. Closing costs typically run 2% to 3% of the cost of the house.

Closing statement
A summation by the seller's attorney identifying various payments and credits that will affect the closing. It is typically sent to your attorney for review.

Commission
A percentage of the sale price paid to the real estate agent. Typically, sellers pay 4% to 6%.

Commitment letter
A bank's official letter approving your loan.

Common charge
A community fee paid by condo and co-op owners to maintain elevators, hallway carpeting, roofs, and any other shared facilities.

Condominium (condo)
A form of shared ownership of a property, typically used in apartments and town houses. A condo owner owns his unit but shares ownership (and upkeep costs) of the roof, cellar, entrance walks, and other common areas.

Contingency clauses
Sections of a contract defining specific situations—such as your inability to secure a mortgage—that can scuttle a deal.

Contract
A legal agreement between you and the seller to transfer ownership in a house for a set price.

Cooperative extension
An academic outreach program that helps impart useful agricultural and forestry research information that can help you make decisions about plants in your yard.

Co-op
A form of shared ownership of property common in New York City and less common in other parts of the country. A co-op owner actually owns shares in the corporation that owns a building. In exchange for those shares, the owner receives a proprietary lease—typically on an apartment.

Counteroffer
A price suggested by a seller that is between your bid and his original asking price.

Covenants
A legal restriction placed on a property. Some discriminatory covenants are still on the books, but federal law prohibits discrimination based on race, religion, sexual orientation, or similar factors. Others, such as a subdivision's covenant disallowing fences, are perfectly legal.

Credit record
An accounting of how you've used your credit, tracked by credit agencies and used by banks to determine the likelihood of your paying a mortgage.

Deed
A document recorded with the local government that denotes your title to a property.

Deposit
Also known as "good-faith money," the portion of the total purchase price that you pay when you sign the contract—typically 5% to 10%.

Electric meter
The power company's device for monitoring your use of electricity.

Equity
The cash value of your house minus the mortgage you still owe on it.

Escrow
The seller's attorney puts your deposit in an escrow account, where it sits until all conditions of the sale are satisfied.

Exclusive listing
An agency's monopoly right to sell a house for a period of time. If another agent brings in the seller, the exclusive agency still receives a portion of the sale.

Feng shui
The ancient Chinese tradition of ordering a room for harmony.

FICO scale
The score, between 300 and 850, given to your credit record by the credit agencies. The higher your FICO score, the better your credit record is.

Forced air
A means of heating or cooling a house by sending air through ducts in the walls.

FSBO

"For sale by owner" is when an individual sells his home without a broker.

Furnace

The source of heat in your home, whether it is gas, oil, or electric.

General contractor

The manager of a construction project who oversees individual tradespeople.

GFCI receptacles

Ground-fault circuit-interrupter receptacles instantly stop sending current to a device when it has short-circuited.

Grout

A filler used between ceramic tiles.

Half-bath

A bathroom with a toilet and sink, but no shower or tub.

Handyman special

A euphemism for a dilapidated house that requires a lot of work.

Hardiness zone

The botanical region of the country where you live. Different plants work best in different zones.

HEPA filters

High-efficiency particulate air filters keep air clean during construction work.

Home equity loan

A loan using the equity in a house as collateral.

Home inspector

A professional hired to inspect a house's condition before purchase.

HVAC

Heating, ventilating, and air-conditioning systems.

Interest rate

The amount, in a percentage, that a bank charges to lend you money.

Leach field

An alternative to sewers, used with septic tanks for getting rid of household waste from drains.

Liabilities

Any obligations, such as a credit-card balance or student loan, that you must pay on a regular basis.

Lien

A legal claim against a property to settle a debt.

Loan period

The number of years over which you repay a mortgage, typically 15 to 30 years. Also called the term.

Lock

Because interest rates vary all the time, banks guarantee—or lock in—a rate to you for a set period of time.

Market value

The final sale price of a house—as opposed to **assessed value.**

Mastic

An adhesive used to secure ceramic tiles to a wall, floor, or countertop.

Mortgage

A bank loan with a house as collateral.

Multiple listing service (MLS)

A way for real estate agents to share houses they are selling (or listing) with agents from other firms that may be representing buyers.

Open house

Listed in the paper, these houses are for sale and are open for certain hours for anyone to visit without an appointment.

Pile

The fabric face of the carpet. There are three main types of pile: loop, cut, and cut and loop.

Pointing

The bonding material that fills the gaps in masonry, similar to grout used between tiles.

Points
One point equals 1% of the mortgage. You can buy points to discount your mortgage.

Prequalification
A bank's process for approving you for a mortgage before you find a house.

Private mortgage insurance (PMI)
A policy that guarantees to pay your mortgage if you don't make the payment, generally required if your mortgage is more than 80 percent of the house's value.

Purchase offer
A legal document used in some states that is the equivalent of a contract, although it is generally written up by your real estate agent.

Real estate taxes
Local government assessments to pay for schools, sewers, and other municipal amenities.

Realtor
A trademark of the National Association of Realtors. Although many people use the term generically, not all real estate agents are Realtors.

Second mortgage
Runs concurrent with your existing mortgage and requires monthly payments.

Septic tank
An alternative means of disposing of waste in areas without sewer lines.

Service panel
Also called a "fuse box" or "breaker box," it divvies up the electrical company's main line to the various circuits in a house. Most new houses include a 200-amp box.

Settling
As the ground under your foundation compacts, it sinks slowly—or settles—into the earth. Settling causes cracks in walls and uneven floors.

Sewer
A municipal system for collecting drain waste from a neighborhood for proper disposal.

Shutoff valve
A means of cutting off the supply of water to your house.

Square feet
The measure used for your home. A room that is 10 feet by 10 feet is 100 square feet.

Survey A review of your property to confirm the buildings on it, generally conducted by the bank during your purchase.

Sweat equity
The value you put into your home by doing improvements yourself rather than hiring outside labor.

Term
The loan period of a mortgage.

Thinset mortar
A base and adhesive that holds ceramic tiles to underlayment.

Title
The right to the possession and ownership in a property.

Title insurance
A policy that banks insist you pick up. A title insurance company researches the deed and confirms that there are no liens against the property.

Tradespeople
Cabinetmakers, plumbers, electricians, and other specialists.

Zoning laws
Local laws that control what can be built on a particular piece of property. Zoning laws generally keep commercial and residential districts separate.

index

National Society of Professional Engineers, 77

negatives, 38–39

neighborhoods
- considerations in, 12–13
- potential negatives of, 38–39
- upkeep of, 38, 39

neighbors, 121

Nest Magazine, 25

new homes, 18–19

90-Second Lawyer Guide to Buying Real Estate, The (Irwin and Ganz), 59

North American Van Lines, 100, 113

O

100 Questions Every First-Time Home Buyer Should Ask (Glink), 25

100 Surefire Improvements to Sell Your House Faster (Woodson), 195

online
- applying for mortgages, 86
- house hunting, 29, 42

open houses, 28, 180, 181

Outdoor Living Room, The (Baker), 159

owners
- buying directly from, 42, 43, 59
- house selling by, 186–187, 195

P

packing, 104–105

padding, 165

paint, 128, 166–167, 176

patios, 148–149

Perfect Palette (Krims), 177

permits, 120–121, 127

personal property, 50

pests, 74–75

pets, 108, 191

planting station, 146

plants, moving, 109

plumbing, 68–69

points, 87, 94

pools, 154–155

prequalification process, 24, 46

previously owned homes, 18–19

prices
- asking, 47, 59–60, 188
- market values, 57
- median house, 8
- new vs. old house, 18

priorities, 8, 10–13

private mortgage insurance, 23

problems
- with deals, 56–57, 194
- found by inspections, 76
- potential, 38–39, 42–43

property taxes, 34–35, 96, 97

Proposition 13, 35

psychographics, 42

public transportation, 13

punch list, 135

purchase offers, 50

R

radiant heat, 133

radon gas, 76

raised ranch, 15

ranch, 15

real estate agents, 30–31, 40, 42, 47, 180, 182–183
  See also commissions

real estate lawyers, 48–49, 187

real property, 50

refinancing, 94–95, 96

relocating, 11

remodeling. *See* improvements/remodeling

Remodeling Online magazine, 137

renovations. *See* improvements/remodeling

rental income, 21, 25

renting, 9, 181

repairs, 76

resale value, 36

retirement funds, 53

rodents, 74–75

the author: up close

Chris Sandlund is an accomplished freelance writer who has published articles on finance, computing, and real estate, among other subjects. In the spring of 2000, he and his wife bought a 120-year-old fixer-upper in Cold Spring, New York. When he isn't writing, he can be found fixing walls, installing tile, or rewiring outlets.

Barbara J. Morgan Publisher, Silver Lining Books

I want to buy a House, Now What?! ™
Barb Chintz Editorial Director
Leonard Vigliarolo Design Director

Lorraine Iannello Managing Editor
David Propson Editor
Anne Marie O'Connor Design Assistant
Monique Boniol Picture Research
Emily Seese Editorial Assistant
Della R. Mancuso Production Manager

Silver Lining Books would like to thank the following consultants for their help in preparing this book:
Mary Croly of Bleakley, Platt, & Schmidt, White Plains, New York
Hope Egan of Ideal Location, Chicago, Illinois
Mike Habib and **Hank Kleis** of Coldwell Banker Real Estate, San Diego, California
David Turner of Randolph Properties, Katonah, New York